BOOK W — CONTENTS

Succeeding in the Workplace and in Life

About *The 21st Century Coach* iv
Meeting the Needs of a Diverse Classroom vi
About 21st Century Skills viii
Teaching 21st Century Skills with *The 21st Century Coach* xii
Strategies for a Flexible Classroom Model xiv

Get started with Lesson 1! *Or create an individualized learning pathway just right for your class on page vi.*

Unit 1 Life Skills
Lesson

73	Taking an Inventory of Your Skills	1
74	Defining Roles and Responsibilities	3
75	Dealing with Change	5
76	Accepting and Giving Feedback	7
77	Resolving Conflicts at Home and in School	9
78	Setting and Meeting Goals	11
79	Asking for Help	13
80	Following Schedules	15
81	Following a Budget	17
82	Furthering Your Education	19
83	Finding and Applying for a Job	21
84	Writing Résumés	23
85	Writing Cover Letters and Thank-You Notes	25

Unit 2 Career Skills
Lesson

86	Making a Good Impression	27
87	Applying Learning Styles	29
88	Being Independent	31
89	Prioritizing Your Work	33
90	Managing Your Time	35
91	Writing a Business Letter	37
92	Writing a Proposal	39
93	Writing a Business E-mail	41
94	Thinking About the Customer	43
95	Resolving Conflicts at Work	45
96	Being Truthful in Business	47
97	Reflecting on Your Work	49

Unit 3 People Skills
Lesson

98	Communicating at Home, School, and Work	51
99	Listening Effectively	53
100	Collaborating at Work	55
101	Influencing People	57
102	Showing Integrity	59
103	Being a Good Leader	61
104	Being a Team Player	63
105	Embracing Differences	65
106	Acting Responsibly	67
107	Inspiring Others to Do Good Work	69
108	Living by a Code of Ethics	71

Graphic Organizers T1

Pathway Placement Survey	Flow Chart
Graphs	Index/Note Cards
Journal	Planner
2-Column Chart	Spreadsheet
3-Column Chart	Storyboard
Checklist	Thought Bubble and Speech Balloon
Computer Screen	Timeline
Concept Map	Venn Diagram

The 21st Century Coach

About *The 21st Century Coach*

The 21st Century Coach will prepare your students for success in the 21st century by giving them the skills and knowledge they will need as citizens, workers, and leaders in this new age. These 21st century skills, as defined by the Partnership for 21st Century Skills, include the key skills that today's students must master to succeed in work and life in today's society.

In this program, you will find engaging, interactive lessons that are designed to motivate students and to build and strengthen their knowledge of 21st century skills. *The 21st Century Coach* program is an efficient learning tool that features:

- **Flexible lesson plans** that help busy teachers easily incorporate 21st century skills instruction.
- Instructional models that provide **clear, concise teacher support.**
- Instructions and activities that are **interesting and relevant** to struggling learners in grades 6–12.
- Content that will **supplement** any core, elective, pullout, or after-school curriculum.

PROGRAM ORGANIZATION
Three Books

The 21st Century Coach program is organized into three different books, each containing 36 lessons. Each focuses on one of the three categories listed in the Partnership for 21st Century Skills Framework and is also based on objectives of other national organizations having interests in preparing students for the future world of work, such as the National Career Development Association.

Improving Creativity, Critical Thinking, Communication, and Collaboration

TEACHER RESOURCE MATERIAL
Lessons 1–36
Topics include:
- Creativity and Innovation
- Critical Thinking and Problem Solving
- Communication and Collaboration

Lesson-specific Graphic Organizers, pp. C1–C16, are referenced at point-of-use in the lessons.

Using Technology, Information, and Media

TEACHER RESOURCE MATERIAL
Lessons 37–72
Topics include:
- Information Literacy
- Media Literacy
- ICT (Information, Communication, Technology) Literacy

Lesson-specific Graphic Organizers, pp. T1–T16, are referenced at point-of-use in the lessons.

Succeeding in the Workplace and in Life

TEACHER RESOURCE MATERIAL
Lessons 73–108
Topics include:
- Life Skills
- Career Skills
- People Skills

Lesson-specific Graphic Organizers, pp. W1–W16, are referenced at point-of-use in the lessons.

See the Book W Contents for more details about the content of the units and individual lessons.

LESSON ORGANIZATION

Each of the 108 lessons features a Teacher Instruction Page and a Student Activity Sheet, designed for flexible use in the classroom.

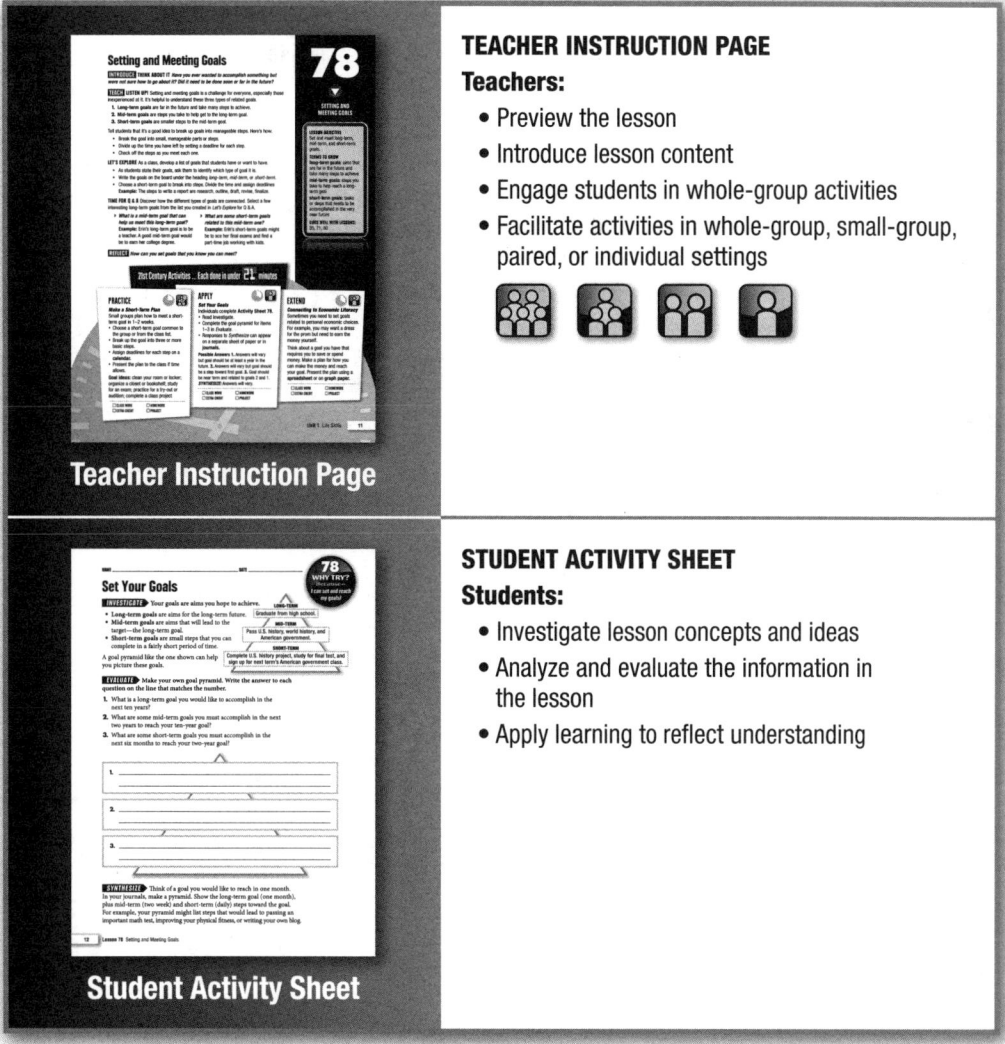

TEACHER INSTRUCTION PAGE
Teachers:
- Preview the lesson
- Introduce lesson content
- Engage students in whole-group activities
- Facilitate activities in whole-group, small-group, paired, or individual settings

STUDENT ACTIVITY SHEET
Students:
- Investigate lesson concepts and ideas
- Analyze and evaluate the information in the lesson
- Apply learning to reflect understanding

Multiple Ways to Teach the Program

The format of 36 lessons per book allows for pacing based on 36 weeks of instruction. Use these tips for presenting the lessons in class:

- **Use Learning Pathway Sequence** Choose from three pathways based on student needs and interests that are determined after each student completes the student Pathway Survey. Each pathway uses one book as a foundation but also integrates supporting lessons from the other two books, maintaining a once-per-week instruction plan with options for more lessons if needed. See pages vi–vii and page W1.
- **Follow Individual Book** If only one book of *The 21st Century Coach* is available for use, teachers may teach one lesson per week for 36 weeks.
- **Teach in 21-minute Increments** Each lesson is composed of teaching sections that can each be completed in under 21 minutes. Following an *Introduce/Teach/Reflect* approach, teachers may instruct the lesson concept in a 21-minute period. To extend class time, teachers may choose from three additional activities, each of which also can be completed within 21 minutes. The remaining activities can be used for additional class work, homework, extra credit, or project work if more time is desired.

Meeting the Needs of a Diverse Classroom

INSTRUCTIONAL AND LEARNING PATHWAYS

This program provides a recommended choice of three learning pathways. Each pathway leads with one book based on the students' strengths and interests, and integrates lessons from the other two books, maintaining a once-per-week instruction plan with options for more as needed. Detailed lesson sequences are provided on the pages that follow for these three learning pathways:

For students who may be headed in the direction of a liberal arts education or career, teach a course with a focus on being creative and innovative in a tech-savvy workplace. Follow the instructional pathway that leads with **Book C,** *Improving Creativity, Critical Thinking, Communication, and Collaboration.*

For students who may pursue careers or degrees in technology, teach a course with a focus on effectively applying technology to information management and communication. Follow the instructional pathway that leads with **Book T,** *Using Technology, Information, and Media.*

For students who may directly enter the workforce or go on to vocational or trade school, teach a course with a focus on the importance of independence and the skills that all businesses expect from their employees. Follow the instructional pathway that leads with **Book W,** *Succeeding in the Workplace and in Life.*

Teaching 21st century skills is most effective when students help set the pathway for learning. Before beginning the program, administer the **Learning Pathways Survey (p. W1)** to your students. This survey is geared toward identifying areas of strength and high interest in students rather than finding the gaps. With this approach, students are motivated to learn skills and concepts that they feel are relevant to them now and in the future.

Use the survey scores to determine which learning pathway best suits your class by looking at the average scores. If you find some students are dominant in a different pathway from the class average, you may want to incorporate a few lessons from another pathway better suited to their needs. This survey can also be used to develop your own customized pathway. Use the books and units in any sequence that you consider most appropriate for your class or for individual students.

To look at the scores in a visual way, plot them on a graph using the graphic organizer **Graph (p. W2).** You can plot the class average scores or, as a math connection, have individuals plot their own.

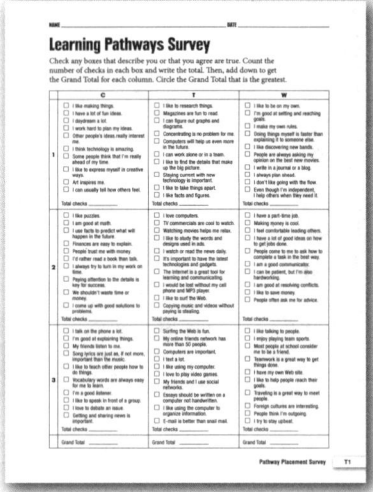

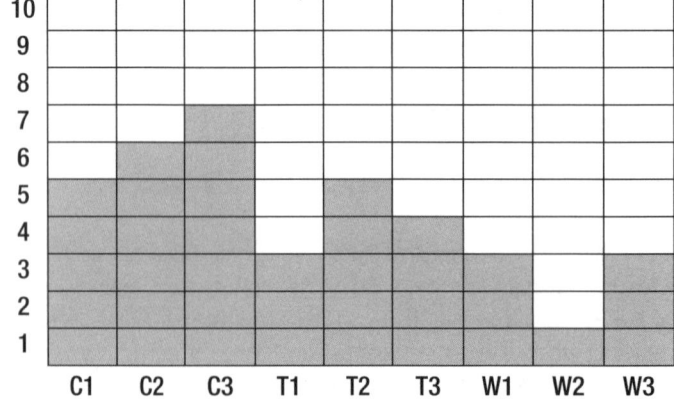

This person will do well following Learning Pathway C.

KEY
- C1 Creator
- C2 Thinker
- C3 Talker
- T1 Data Minded
- T2 Mediaphile
- T3 Techy
- W1 Indie
- W2 The "Boss"
- W3 Networker

Meeting the Needs of a Diverse Classroom

LEARNING PATHWAY LESSON SEQUENCES

WK	C — Unit 1: Creativity and Innovation	T — Unit 1: Information Literacy	W — Life Skills
1	C1 Recognizing Innovation	T37 Defining Types of Information	W74 Defining Roles and Responsibilities
2	C3 Generating Ideas	C2 Thinking Like an Innovator	W75 Dealing with Change
3	C4 Organizing Ideas	T38 Finding Sources of Information	W76 Accepting and Giving Feedback
4	C5 Refining Ideas	C11 Finding Opportunities for Creativity	W77 Resolving Conflicts at Home and in School
5	C6 Turning an Idea into a Storyboard	T40 Making Information Accessible to the Impaired	W78 Setting and Meeting Goals
6	C8 Turning an Idea into Creative Writing	T44 Searching the Internet	T38 Finding Sources of Information
7	T57 Creating Ads	T70 Guidelines for Using Databases	C3 Generating Ideas
8	T58 Creating Newsletters	W78 Setting and Meeting Goals	C4 Organizing Ideas
9	T59 Creating Web Sites	W80 Following Schedules	C8 Turning an Idea into Creative Writing
10	T60 Writing Scripts	T45 Using Information Ethically	W80 Following Schedules
11	C34 Working Creatively in a Team	W92 Writing a Proposal	W81 Following a Budget
12	C12 Protecting Ideas	C12 Protecting Ideas	W83 Finding and Applying for a Job

WK	Unit 2: Critical Thinking and Problem Solving	Unit 2: Media Literacy	Career Skills
13	C13 Thinking Critically	T49 Defining Media	W86 Making a Good Impression
14	C15 Analyzing Cause and Effect	T50 Comparing Forms of Media	W90 Managing Your Time
15	C41 Reading Visual Information	T51 Analyzing Commercial Media	C13 Thinking Critically
16	C20 Considering Point of View	T52 Analyzing Political Media	W91 Writing a Business Letter
17	C21 Asking Questions	W101 Influencing People	W93 Writing a Business E-mail
18	C22 Synthesizing Information	T54 Applying Values	T69 Using Word Processors
19	C23 Making Good Decisions	C3 Generating Ideas	W92 Writing a Proposal
20	W92 Writing a Proposal	C4 Organizing Ideas	T71 Guidelines for Using Spreadsheets
21	W94 Thinking About the Customer	C5 Refining Ideas	W94 Thinking About the Customer
22	W95 Resolving Conflicts at Work	T57 Creating Ads	T55 Seeing Points of View
23	W96 Being Truthful in Business	T58 Creating Newsletters	W95 Resolving Conflicts at Work
24	W97 Reflecting on Your Work	T59 Creating Web Sites	W97 Reflecting on Your Work

WK	Unit 3: Communication and Collaboration	Unit 3: ICT Literacy	People Skills
25	C25 Communicating Ideas	W98 Communicating at Home, School, and Work	W98 Communicating at Home, School, and Work
26	W76 Accepting and Giving Feedback	T67 Being Safe on the Internet	C26 Communicating Without Words
27	C28 Communicating to Inform	T64 Networking	W99 Listening Effectively
28	C29 Communicating to Persuade	T65 Blogging	T64 Networking
29	W86 Making a Good Impression	T69 Using Word Processors	W100 Collaborating at Work
30	W107 Inspiring Others to Do Good Work	W91 Writing a Business E-mail	W102 Showing Integrity
31	C34 Working Creatively in a Team	T71 Guidelines for Using Spreadsheets	W103 Being a Good Leader
32	W78 Setting and Meeting Goals	W82 Following a Budget	W104 Being a Team Player
33	C30 Preparing a Presentation	T66 Using Digital Media Technology	W106 Acting Responsibly
34	T72 Guidelines for Using Presentation Software	T72 Guidelines for Using Presentation Software	C31 Giving a Speech
35	T66 Using Digital Media Technology	T48 Sharing Information	T72 Guidelines for Using Presentation Software
36	C36 Collaborating and Presenting Together	W108 Living by a Code of Ethics	W108 Living By a Code of Ethics

KEY: C=Liberal Arts/Creativity/Innovation   T=Technology/Media/Information   W=Workplace/Business School//Life Skills

The 21st Century Coach

About 21st Century Skills

The 21st century is a digital age marked by rapid changes in technology and a globally competitive economy. To succeed, students still need strong reading, writing, and computation skills and knowledge of core subjects like language arts, mathematics, science, and social studies. But traditional literacies and subject-matter knowledge are not enough. Schools need to prepare students for the kinds of responsibilities they will hold as employees, heads of households, and citizens. *The 21st Century Coach* attempts to bridge the gap between coursework and real work by focusing on real-world skills and applications.

DEFINING 21ST CENTURY SKILLS

Through real-world applications, 21st century skills help students transfer their knowledge of core subjects and develop these and other new competencies. The following competencies make up the framework that defines 21st century skills:

Creativity and Innovation Skills
- Generate, evaluate, and explain new ideas
- Implement new ideas to accomplish goals

Critical Thinking and Problem Solving Skills
- Make inferences, comparisons, and cause-effect analyses
- Analyze arguments and evaluate their validity
- Use systems thinking to recognize and solve problems
- Use tools to make informed decisions

Communication and Collaboration Skills
- Use spoken and written messages to inform and persuade
- Use active listening to understand others' thoughts and feelings
- Gather, interpret, and evaluate diverse viewpoints
- Work harmoniously with people of different cultures and backgrounds

Information, Media, and Technology Skills
- Use digital technology to locate sources of information
- Evaluate the accuracy and truthfulness of information sources
- Use tools to organize and manage the flow of information
- Use information sources responsibly and ethically
- Analyze the purpose of media messages
- Evaluate the validity of claims made in media messages
- Use technology to create effective multimedia messages

Life and Career Skills
- Work effectively in teams, both as a leader and as a team member
- Effectively give and accept feedback
- Manage time and money to meet personal and work goals
- Work independently to complete tasks on schedule
- Use conflict management techniques to resolve interpersonal conflicts

REINFORCING SKILLS IN BOOK W

Young people want their work in school to be meaningful and relevant to their lives. Learning 21st century life and career skills helps students see the connection between what they do in school and what they will need to do in the home and at work. Students need skills in setting short- and long-term goals, finding and understanding information about investment products, and making realistic budgets and savings plans. To navigate the career-planning process and to maintain successful careers, students need the 21st century skills of adaptability, decision-making, planning, and self-reflection. Young people need to understand global issues, cultural differences, and differing and sometimes conflicting viewpoints to work collaboratively with people of diverse backgrounds. These 21st century skills should be part of their education.

Correlation to Partnership for 21st Century Skills

Life and Career Skills			Book W Lessons
Flexibility and Adaptability	Adapt to Change	Adapt to varied roles, jobs responsibilities, schedules and contexts	74, 80, 81
		Work effectively in a climate of ambiguity and changing priorities	75, 79
	Be Flexible	Incorporate feedback effectively	76
		Deal positively with praise, setbacks and criticism	76
		Understand, negotiate and balance diverse views and beliefs to reach workable solutions, particularly in multi-cultural environments	77, 95
Initiative and Self-Direction	Manage Goals and Time	Set goals with tangible and intangible success criteria	73, 78
		Balance tactical (short-term) and strategic (long-term) goals	78
		Utilize time and manage workload efficiently	89, 90
	Work Independently	Monitor, define, prioritize and complete tasks without direct oversight	88
	Be Self-Directed Learners	Go beyond basic mastery of skills and/or curriculum to explore and expand one's own learning and opportunities to gain expertise	82, 87
		Demonstrate initiative to advance skill levels towards a professional level	73, 83, 84, 85
		Demonstrate commitment to learning as a lifelong process	82
		Reflect critically on past experiences in order to inform future progress	87, 97
Social and Cross-Cultural Skills	Interact Effectively with Others	Know when it is appropriate to listen and when to speak	98, 99
		Conduct oneself in a respectable, professional manner	86
	Work Effectively in Diverse Teams	Respect cultural differences and work effectively with people from a range of social and cultural backgrounds	105
		Respond open-mindedly to different ideas and values	101, 105
		Leverage social and cultural differences to create new ideas and increase both innovation and quality of work	101
Productivity and Accountability	Manage Projects	Set and meet goals, even in the face of obstacles and competing pressures	95
		Prioritize, plan and manage work to achieve the intended result	89, 90, 94
	Produce Results	Demonstrate additional attributes associated with producing high quality products including the abilities to: work positively and ethically; manage time and projects effectively; multi-task; participate actively, as well as be reliable and punctual; present oneself professionally and with proper etiquette; collaborate and cooperate effectively with teams; respect and appreciate team diversity; be accountable for results	91, 92, 93, 96, 100, 104
Leadership and Responsibility	Guide and Lead Others	Use interpersonal and problem-solving skills to influence and guide others toward a goal	95, 103
		Leverage strengths of others to accomplish a common goal	103
		Inspire others to reach their very best via example and selflessness	107
		Demonstrate integrity and ethical behavior in using influence and power	106, 108
	Be Responsible to Others	Act responsibly with the interests of the larger community in mind	102

From *21st Century Student Outcomes,* Partnership for 21st Century Skills, December 2009.

UNDERSTANDING 21ST CENTURY THEMES

Five essential interdisciplinary themes, or learning outcomes, inform 21st century skills. These outcomes represent new kinds of literacies that students will need in order to thrive in the world beyond the classroom.

- **Global Awareness,** or an understanding of other countries and cultures. This includes an awareness of global issues as well as the ability to learn from and work with people of diverse cultures and backgrounds.
- **Financial, Economic, Business, and Entrepreneurial Literacy,** or an understanding of the role that the economy plays in personal and business financial decisions. This includes the ability to use entrepreneurial skills to work more productively and create career opportunities.
- **Civic Literacy,** or an understanding of governmental processes. This includes the ability to work within existing processes to participate in government at all levels as well as to help shape processes to improve government.
- **Health Literacy,** or an understanding of how to find and use health information and services. This includes the ability to make informed decisions that enhance the health and safety of the individual, family, and community.
- **Environmental Literacy,** or an understanding of the natural world and people's impact on it. This includes an understanding of environmental issues and ways to generate and measure the effectiveness of solutions.

THEME-BASED PROJECTS IN BOOK W

The final Extend activity of each lesson connects to one of the five interdisciplinary themes. Use the following chart to locate project-based activities on each theme.

Lesson Number	Theme	Lesson Number	Theme
73	Civic	91	Business
74	Business	92	Health
75	Health	93	Civic
76	Civic	94	Business
77	Health	95	Global
78	Economic	96	Business
79	Health	97	Environmental
80	Business	98	Global
81	Financial	99	Civic
82	Financial	100	Civic
83	Business	101	Environmental
84	Business	102	Global
85	Business	103	Health
86	Global	104	Entrepreneurial
87	Health	105	Global
88	Business	106	Environmental
89	Environmental	107	Health
90	Health	108	Civic

About 21st Century Skills

INTEGRATING 21st CENTURY SKILLS WITH CORE CONTENT AREAS

Because 21st century skills are interdisciplinary in nature, they can be integrated into virtually any existing curriculum. At the same time, some skills correlate more closely with certain content areas than with others. Use the following suggestions as starting points to spark ideas of your own.

Content Area	Corresponding Book W Lessons	
Language Arts Life and career skills go hand in hand with the language arts curriculum. For example, lessons on giving and accepting feedback can be integrated into peer evaluations of writing, and lessons on composing business correspondence into writing instruction.	73 Taking an Inventory of Your Skills 76 Accepting and Giving Feedback 77 Resolving Conflicts at Home and in School 82 Furthering Your Education 83 Finding and Applying for a Job 84 Writing Résumés 85 Writing Cover Letters and Thank-You Notes	86 Making a Good Impression 91 Writing a Business Letter 92 Writing a Proposal 93 Writing a Business E-mail 98 Communicating at Home, School, and Work
Mathematics Project-based activities that require math skills are an excellent way to integrate 21st century skills into the mathematics classroom. For example, you might challenge students to use an electronic spreadsheet to create a project schedule or budget or to use a rating points system to prioritize their work.	73 Taking an Inventory of Your Skills 79 Asking for Help 80 Following Schedules 81 Following a Budget 87 Applying Learning Styles	89 Prioritizing Your Work 90 Managing Your Time 97 Reflecting on Your Work 99 Listening Effectively 106 Acting Responsibly
Science There are many opportunities to integrate 21st century skills into the science classroom. For example, you might integrate lessons on dealing with change into discussions of technology or lessons on setting and meeting goals into discussions of science projects.	75 Dealing with Change 78 Setting and Meeting Goals 80 Following Schedules 81 Following a Budget 82 Furthering Your Education	87 Applying Learning Styles 88 Being Independent 92 Writing a Proposal 102 Showing Integrity 108 Living by a Code of Ethics
Social Studies Social studies curriculum lends itself to 21st century skills. For example, lessons on leadership can be integrated into studies of world leaders, and lessons on being a team player into discussions of group projects.	74 Defining Roles and Responsibilities 75 Dealing with Change 89 Prioritizing Your Work 94 Thinking About the Customer 95 Resolving Conflicts at Work 96 Being Truthful in Business	100 Collaborating at Work 101 Influencing People 103 Being a Great Leader 104 Being a Team Player 105 Embracing Differences 107 Inspiring Others to Do Good Work

The 21st Century Coach

Teaching 21st Century Skills with *The 21st Century Coach*

THE TEACHER INSTRUCTION PAGE

This program was designed so each lesson has the teacher and student component at point of use. The Teacher Instruction Page provides the primary information needed to meet the lesson objective. Lesson sequence is predictable but flexible in its application in the classroom.

See pages xiv–xv for a more detailed walkthrough of the Teacher Instruction Page.

Introduce with THINK ABOUT IT.
Set the stage for the content learning to come.
Tip: Ask the question aloud and ask volunteers to answer.

Teach with LET'S EXPLORE.
Engage students in active content learning using a whole-group activity.

Have students REFLECT on what they learned.
Ask for responses aloud in class, or have students respond in their Journal.

PRACTICE, APPLY, or EXTEND with 21st Century Activities.
Complete each in under 21 minutes.

Setting and Meeting Goals

INTRODUCE **THINK ABOUT IT** *Have you ever wanted to accomplish something but were not sure how to go about it? Did it need to be done soon or far in the future?*

TEACH **LISTEN UP!** Setting and meeting goals is a challenge for everyone, especially those inexperienced at it. It's helpful to understand these three types of related goals.

1. **Long-term goals** are far in the future and take many steps to achieve.
2. **Mid-term goals** are steps you take to help get to the long-term goal.
3. **Short-term goals** are smaller steps to the mid-term goal.

Tell students that it's a good idea to break up goals into manageable steps. Here's how:
- Break the goal into small, manageable parts or steps.
- Divide up the time you have left by setting a deadline for each step.
- Check off the steps as you meet each one.

LET'S EXPLORE As a class, develop a list of goals that students have or want to have.
- As students state their goals, ask them to identify which type of goal it is.
- Write the goals on the board under the heading *long-term, mid-term,* or *short-term.*
- Choose a short-term goal to break into steps. Divide the time and assign deadlines
  Example: The steps to write a report are research, outline, draft, revise, finalize.

TIME FOR Q & A Discover how the different types of goals are connected. Select a few interesting long-term goals from the list you created in *Let's Explore* for Q & A.

▶ **What is a mid-term goal that can help us meet this long-term goal?**
Example: Erin's long-term goal is to be a teacher. A good mid-term goal would be to earn her college degree.

▶ **What are some short-term goals related to this mid-term one?**
Example: Erin's short-term goals might be to ace her final exams and find a part-time job working with kids.

REFLECT *How can you set goals that you know you can meet?*

78

▼

SETTING AND MEETING GOALS

LESSON OBJECTIVE
Set and meet long-term, mid-term, and short-term goals.

TERMS TO KNOW
long-term goals: aims that are far in the future and take many steps to achieve
mid-term goals: steps you take to help reach a long-term goal
short-term goals: tasks or steps that needs to be accomplished in the very near future

GOES WELL WITH LESSONS: 35, 71, 80

Preview the lesson.
Provide lesson objective and key terms at a glance.
Tip: Pair lesson with complementary lessons in the program.

21st Century Activities ... Each done in under 21 minutes

PRACTICE
Make a Short-Term Plan
Small groups plan how to meet a short-term goal in 1–2 weeks.
- Choose a short-term goal common to the group or from the class list.
- Break up the goal into three or more basic steps.
- Assign deadlines for each step on a **calendar**.
- Present the plan to the class if time allows.

Goal ideas: clean your room or locker; organize a closet or bookshelf; study for an exam; practice for a try-out or audition; complete a class project

☐ CLASS WORK ☐ HOMEWORK
☐ EXTRA CREDIT ☐ PROJECT

APPLY
Set Your Goals
Individuals complete **Activity Sheet 78.**
- Read investigate.
- Complete the goal pyramid for items 1–3 in *Evaluate.*
- Responses to *Synthesize* can appear on a separate sheet of paper or in **journals.**

Possible Answers 1. Answers will vary but goal should be at least a year in the future. **2.** Answers will vary but goal should be a step toward first goal. **3.** Goal should be near term and related to goals 2 and 1.
SYNTHESIZE: Answers will vary.

☐ CLASS WORK ☐ HOMEWORK
☐ EXTRA CREDIT ☐ PROJECT

EXTEND
Connecting to Economic Literacy
Sometimes you need to set goals related to personal economic choices. For example, you may want a dress for the prom but need to earn the money yourself.

Think about a goal you have that requires you to save or spend money. Make a plan for how you can make the money and reach your goal. Present the plan using a **spreadsheet** or on **graph paper.**

☐ CLASS WORK ☐ HOMEWORK
☐ EXTRA CREDIT ☐ PROJECT

Select best group size and time for your class.
Use icons to identify group sizes as large, small, paired, or individual. Plan for activities that vary from 5 to 20 minutes.

Assign activities with flexible options.
Assign in class, as a project, for homework, or as extra credit.

Unit 1 Life Skills

THE STUDENT ACTIVITY SHEET

The reverse side of every lesson's Teacher Instruction Page contains a reproducible Student Activity Sheet that provides a way for students to apply what they've learned. You may also use the Student Activity Sheet as a formative assessment tool.

See page xvi for a more detailed walkthrough of the Student Activity Sheet.

INVESTIGATE lesson concepts and ideas.

Provides easy to follow, highly visual text for struggling learners reading at a 3rd to 4th grade level.

Tip: Allow time for silent or choral reading of instructions and passages.

Students learn to EVALUATE.

Allows for practical application of students' new knowledge.

Tip: Provide enlarged copies of an Activity Sheet if students are asked to mark it up or draw.

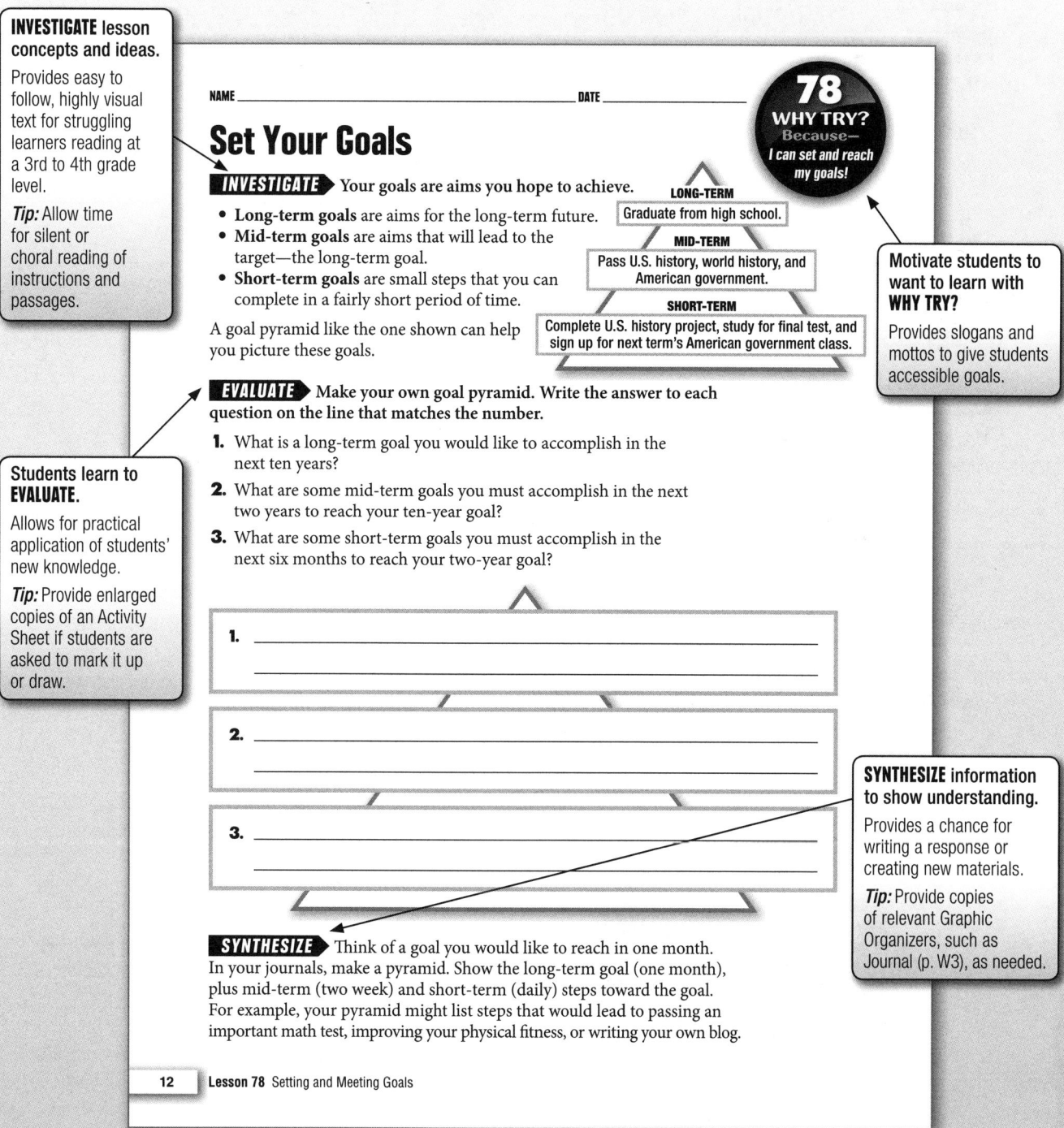

NAME _____ DATE _____

Set Your Goals

78 WHY TRY? Because— I can set and reach my goals!

INVESTIGATE Your goals are aims you hope to achieve.

- **Long-term goals** are aims for the long-term future.
- **Mid-term goals** are aims that will lead to the target—the long-term goal.
- **Short-term goals** are small steps that you can complete in a fairly short period of time.

LONG-TERM: Graduate from high school.
MID-TERM: Pass U.S. history, world history, and American government.
SHORT-TERM: Complete U.S. history project, study for final test, and sign up for next term's American government class.

A goal pyramid like the one shown can help you picture these goals.

EVALUATE Make your own goal pyramid. Write the answer to each question on the line that matches the number.

1. What is a long-term goal you would like to accomplish in the next ten years?
2. What are some mid-term goals you must accomplish in the next two years to reach your ten-year goal?
3. What are some short-term goals you must accomplish in the next six months to reach your two-year goal?

1. _____
2. _____
3. _____

SYNTHESIZE Think of a goal you would like to reach in one month. In your journals, make a pyramid. Show the long-term goal (one month), plus mid-term (two week) and short-term (daily) steps toward the goal. For example, your pyramid might list steps that would lead to passing an important math test, improving your physical fitness, or writing your own blog.

12   Lesson 78 Setting and Meeting Goals

Motivate students to want to learn with WHY TRY?

Provides slogans and mottos to give students accessible goals.

SYNTHESIZE information to show understanding.

Provides a chance for writing a response or creating new materials.

Tip: Provide copies of relevant Graphic Organizers, such as Journal (p. W3), as needed.

The 21st Century Coach   xiii

Strategies for a Flexible Classroom Model

TEACHING THE LESSONS

Each lesson in *The 21st Century Coach* is designed to be taught in a manner that meets the needs of your classroom. The instruction section can be taught in under 21 minutes. Each student activity can be completed in under 21 minutes. You can plan for a 40-minute class or break up instruction as needed. As you read the following pages, think about how you can adjust the lessons to meet your needs and the needs of your students. Use this sample lesson plan as a guide.

Lesson Plan 3	Day	Time	Description	Prep/Notes
INTRODUCE	1	3 min	*Think About It* question on the board; share responses	*Journals night before*
TEACH	1	15 min	• *Listen Up!* lecture —Explore writing new goals using a 3-column chart graphic organizer. • Pairs work together in Q & A	• *Copy 3-Column Chart p. W5*
REFLECT	2		Answer in journals	*Homework*
ACTIVITIES	2	15 min	*Set Your Goals* activity in small groups	• *Copy Activity 78, Journals, p. W3*

INTRODUCE

Motivate students before teaching the content using one or more of these techniques:

- Identify the **Lesson Objective** by completing the sentence, "When you've completed this lesson, you will be able to…"
- Review the **Terms to Know** and have students record them in a Word Log or Journal.
- Pose the **Think About It** question and solicit responses as a discussion-starter. You may want to have students respond to the question in their Journal ahead of time, so they have a chance to think about it on their own and are prepared to discuss it the next day.
- Post the *Why Try?* motto from the Student Activity Sheet, and briefly discuss it with students before beginning the lesson.

TEACH

Instruct concepts using a three-pronged approach: presenting ideas labeled *Listen Up!;* whole-class work labeled *Let's Explore;* refining ideas labeled *Think, Pair, Share; Time For Q & A; Reverse Q & A; Play These Roles;* or *Interview Your Peers.*

▶ **First, present the concepts — LISTEN UP!**

This section details the main concepts of the lesson to be used during exposition or lecture-like presentation. It is designed to provide the information needed, with minimal instruction on methodology, leaving much to the teacher's discretion. Here are some techniques to use with *Listen Up!*:

- Allow at least 5–10 minutes for this part of the lesson.
- Use appropriate content as a script and read it verbatim to the class.
- Pose italicized questions and solicit responses orally or have volunteers write on the board.
- Write bulleted ideas on the board or other device as you discuss each one. You might use a 3-column chart (**3-Column Chart, p. W5**) or other graphic organizer as a way to organize the information.
- Discuss each numbered or bulleted step in a process using a flow chart. You might provide **Flow Chart (p. W9)** for students to use when taking notes.
- Emphasize bolded **Terms To Know** used in context. Refer to the margin for definitions.

Strategies for a Flexible Classroom Model

▶ Next, the WHOLE CLASS engages in a large-group activity — **LET'S EXPLORE**

This section provides for active discussion, focused around a whole-class activity. Use it to engage students in active content learning with these techniques:

- Allow at least 5–10 minutes for this part of the lesson.
- Prepare for this activity by copying graphic organizers or gathering materials ahead of time.
- Each activity is different, but it often involves brainstorming ideas with students.
- Assign roles, such as recorder and timekeeper, to students and then switch roles.
- Use a chalkboard, white board, chart paper, overhead, or smart board to display ideas for all to see. Use different colors to distinguish categories when appropriate.
- After brainstorming, use the prompt questions to analyze and discuss the materials generated by the group.
- Save the content you've generated. It is often used in other activities later in the lesson. You might ask volunteers to enter the content on a computer or transcribe it onto note paper.
- Have students record the ideas in their Journal for further analysis.

▶ Then, **SMALL GROUPS** get into more details…

One of the following activities will be specified in each lesson, but you can mix and match types of activities to fit your students' unique learning styles. For example, if your students tend to learn best through kinesthetic learning, transform a Q & A into role-playing using one of the strategies that follow.

▶ **THINK, PAIR, SHARE** presents a topic to be discussed between student pairs.

- Pairs are given time to think and discuss an issue. Then they share their response/idea/solutions with a larger group.
- Encourage students to think independently and then share ideas.
- Provide materials to be used for presenting ideas.

▶ **TIME FOR Q & A** uses a question-and-answer discovery approach to build meaning.

- Pose the questions to the students as a springboard for discussion.
- Play a game in which answers are given and the questions are sought, similar to a popular game show.
- Add to the base of questions by making ones relevant to the current core curriculum.

▶ **REVERSE Q & A** prompts students to ask their own questions to encourage critical thinking and discovery.

- Invite questions from students on the topic by asking: *What do you already know? What do you want to know? Which details are most important? What is not making sense?*
- If students get stuck, offer the example questions provided.

▶ **PLAY THESE ROLES** challenges students to act out situations they may potentially face related to the topic.

- Explain the role-playing scenario giving examples as needed.
- Choose volunteers to act it out. Assign roles if students are reluctant.
- Have students switch roles to see both sides.
- Role-plays can be observed by the whole class or done with smaller groups.
- Discuss the role-play with observers by using the provided questions as a guide.

▶ **INTERVIEW YOUR PEERS** provides topics for the basis of mock interviews.

- Present the interview topic, giving examples as needed.
- Allow time for students to plan their questions.
- Have partners interview each other.
- Invite pairs to share the ideas collected with the class and discuss them.
- Encourage students to present different opinions and points of view.
- Extend the activity by having students perform multiple interviews and compile a written summary for extra credit or homework.

REFLECT

Have students reflect on the content they have learned by posing this question. They can respond in a variety of formats.

- Ask for oral responses in class as an ongoing assessment to check for understanding.
- Write the question on the board and have students respond in their Journal for homework.
- Use a Think-Pair-Share activity to have students respond collaboratively.
- Spark a debate using the question as the basis for a Pro-Con analysis.
- Provide copies of the **Journal** graphic organizer on **page W3** so students can keep a Journal notebook.
- Create a class Journal or bulletin board featuring responses and reflections.

The 21st Century Coach

21st Century Activities

The bottom portion of each lesson provides related activity options: Practice, Apply, and Extend. Each can be competed in less than 21 minutes. Choose one or do them all based on your available time and lesson plan. They can be used for class work, homework, extra credit, or projects.

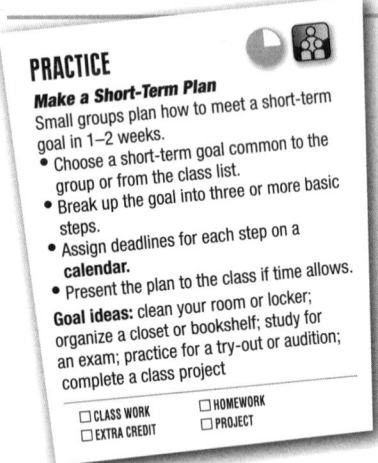

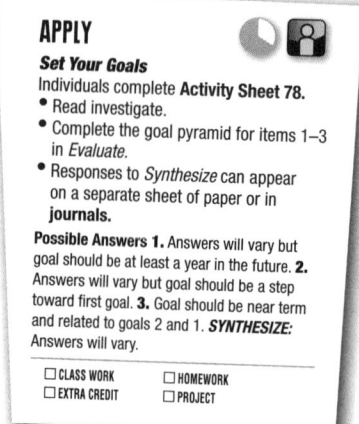

PRACTICE reinforces the content of the lesson through active learning.

- Icons identify the group size as large, small, or individual.
- The clock icon estimates the time you should allow for completion of the task.
- Any materials you might need are boldfaced for ease in planning.
- Steps are bulleted and may be reproduced for students on note cards or on the board as needed.
- Each activity is different. Be sure to review with students the directions in the individual lessons before they begin.

APPLY allows students to apply what they have learned with minimal instruction from the teacher by utilizing a reproducible activity sheet.

- Directions for teacher preparation, group sizes, and duration are provided.
- Teacher Instruction Page provides guidance for discussing or assessing students' activity sheets.
- Use the possible answers as guides, but bear in mind students' unique perspectives.
- Student Activity Sheets should be copied for each student in the class regardless of group size.
- The passages and instructions on the worksheets are leveled at grades 3–4 based on the Lexile scale.
- Student Activity Sheets may reference reproducible graphic organizers, such as the Journal and Concept Map. These Graphic Organizers can be found on pages W1–W16 of this book.
- These Student Activity Sheets include three sections:

EXTEND provides students with real-world applications of information.

- Use these activities to connect to a 21st century theme. See page x for more on themes.
- The first paragraph explains the connection, so be sure to share this with students.
- Encourage creativity and ingenuity by allowing flexibility with the types of products created.
- Integrate 21st century skills into core content areas by adapting to your current course of study.

INVESTIGATIONS provide information for students based on a portion of the teaching instruction and lesson contents. They usually provide a passage or other type of example to be read and absorbed.

ACTIVITIES create an opportunity for a practical application of students' new knowledge in an accessible format. Each is based on a higher-order thinking activity. Students interact with the text by marking their answers on the page.

RESPONSES act as a conclusion to the worksheet and a way to reflect on learning. Each response may include a written response for journals or the creation of other materials that relate to the lesson content.

Strategies for a Flexible Classroom Model

Taking an Inventory of Your Skills

73

TAKING AN INVENTORY OF YOUR SKILLS

INTRODUCE **THINK ABOUT IT** *Did you know that the things you are good at might be skills that can make you a success in life?*

TEACH **LISTEN UP!** Everyone has skills that make him or her a success in different areas of life. There are many types of skills. Here are several:

- **School skills** include studying, reading, math, and other learning skills.
- **Creative skills** include writing, painting, and making music or other art.
- **Communication skills** include working well with others, clearly explaining your ideas by writing and speaking, and sometimes even helping others resolve conflicts.
- **Technology skills** include using computers to create, write, and communicate.

It's good to identify your strong skills, and to know the skills you want to develop. Here's how:

- Think about activities in which you do well and that you enjoy.
- Identify the skills a person would require to excel in those activities.
- Do the same for activities in which you would like to excel.

LET'S EXPLORE As a class, develop a list of skills that students have or want to have.

- As students state the skills, ask them to identify which type of skill it is.
- Write the skills on the board under the headings *School, Creative, Communications,* or *Technology.* Ask students to identify new headings, if necessary.

TIME FOR Q & A Discover how to gain and improve skills. Select a few interesting skills from the list you created in *Let's Explore* as the focus of Q & A.

▸ *How could someone who has this skill improve on it?*
Someone already good at math could improve her skill by doing extra practice problems.

▸ *How could someone without this skill gain it?*
Someone who wants to be a singer could take singing lessons.

REFLECT *How can you use the skills you already have to help you succeed in life?*

LESSON OBJECTIVE
Demonstrate initiative to advance skill levels and set goals.

TERMS TO KNOW
communication skills: abilities that help you when speaking, writing, presenting, and sharing information with others
creative skills: abilities that help you be creative and innovative
school skills: abilities that help you succeed in school
technology skills: abilities that involve using computers

GOES WELL WITH LESSONS:
13, 43, 78

21st Century Activities ... Each done in under **21** minutes

PRACTICE
Skills Matching
Pairs create a poster that highlights students' skills.

- Students write their names on 2 **Index Cards (p. W10).** On one card, they write a skill they have; on the other they write a skill they'd like to have.
- Adhere the note cards on **butcher paper.** Have students locate a peer who has the skill they want to have.
- The pair then discusses how the skill owner gained that skill and lays out goals for the new student to do the same.

☐ CLASS WORK ☐ HOMEWORK
☐ EXTRA CREDIT ☐ PROJECT

APPLY
Create a Learning Skills Inventory
Individuals complete **Activity Sheet 73.**
- Students will complete the chart and answer the *Evaluate* questions.
- Distribute **Journal (p. W3)** for students to respond to *Analyze*.

Possible Answers Answers to **EVALUATE** and **ANALYZE** will vary, based on level of individual skills. However, answers should show careful reflection of personal skills.

☐ CLASS WORK ☐ HOMEWORK
☐ EXTRA CREDIT ☐ PROJECT

EXTEND
Connect to Civic Literacy
Everyone has the ability to be a great civic leader some day, but being a leader requires developing certain skills.

Choose a local, state, or national civic leader who has recently been in the news for creating positive change. Identify the skills that person has that makes him or her a great leader. Present your findings to the class in an oral presentation. Support your presentation with a **visual aid**, such as a poster about or electronic images of the leader.

☐ CLASS WORK ☐ HOMEWORK
☐ EXTRA CREDIT ☐ PROJECT

Unit 1 Life Skills   1

NAME _____ DATE _____

Create a Learning Skills Inventory

73 WHY TRY? Because— I have great skills!

INVESTIGATE Your skills allow you to succeed.

You have many different kinds of skills. In this activity, you will focus on **school skills**. Think about how strong or weak your learning skills are. Check one box after each skill area. Be honest! This activity will help you improve your learning skills.

SKILLS INVENTORY

	Excellent	Good	Fair	Poor
1. Reading speed				
2. Reading comprehension				
3. Listening				
4. Memory				
5. Following directions				
6. Computer skills				
7. Classroom note-taking				
8. Internet research				
9. Basic library skills				
10. Writing papers				
11. Studying for tests				
12. Test-taking				

EVALUATE Review your responses on the Skills Inventory chart. Then write the answer to each question below on the line provided.

1. Which study skill areas do you now feel are your strongest?

   _____

2. Which study skill areas do you now feel you need to improve?

   _____

ANALYZE Analyze your skills and write how to improve.

Look at your answer from question number 2 above. In your Journal, write each skill you feel you need to improve. Then, for each skill, write at least two things you could do to improve that skill. Set goals for yourself to improve your skills.

2   Lesson 73 Taking an Inventory of Your Skills   © 2011 Saddleback Educational Publishing

Defining Roles and Responsibilities

74

INTRODUCE **THINK ABOUT IT** *What roles and responsibilities do you have in your life?*

TEACH **LISTEN UP!** People have many different roles in many different situations, such as at home, school, and at work.

- **Roles** are the jobs that people have in a given situation.
- **Responsibilities** are the tasks or actions involved in doing a job.
- **Skills** are the abilities people have that help them to do a job.

Tell students that in their **roles** as students, some **responsibilities** are to do homework and study. Ask: *What **skills** help you to do these responsibilities?*

LET'S EXPLORE As a class, create a mind map of roles and responsibilities of people at school.

- On the board, use the **Concept Map (p. W8)** and place *School* in the center of it.
- Ask students to name roles of people at school, such as *teacher, principal, student, cafeteria worker,* and *janitor*. Write these in circles extended from the center circle.
- Ask students to name the responsibilities involved in these roles. Write these in circles extended from each role circle.

TIME FOR Q & A Discover the skills involved in various roles. For the Q & A, select a few roles from the mind map you created in *Let's Explore*.

▶ *What are some skills a cafeteria worker needs?*
Examples: the skills of knowing how to order the right quantities of food and cooking

▶ *What are some skills a teacher needs?*
Examples: the skills of explaining lessons well, reading well, and organizing materials

REFLECT *What roles and responsibilities do you have at home?*

DEFINING ROLES AND RESPONSIBILITIES

LESSON OBJECTIVE
Adapt to varied roles, jobs responsibilities, schedules, and contexts.

TERMS TO KNOW
responsibilities: the tasks or actions involved in doing a job
roles: the jobs that people have in a given situation
skills: abilities people have that help them to do a job

GOES WELL WITH LESSONS:
14, 48, 104

21st Century Activities ... Each done in under 21 minutes

PRACTICE
Roles and Responsibilities Charades
On **Index Cards (p. W10)**, write the names of different roles, such as mother, doctor, teacher, manager, student, and so on.
- Divide the class in half.
- A person from each team acts out the responsibilities of the role on his/her card.
- That person's team members attempt to guess the role.
- Be mindful that there might be more than one right answer (i.e., a mother's responsibilities could also apply to a day-care worker).

☐ CLASS WORK ☐ HOMEWORK
☐ EXTRA CREDIT ☐ PROJECT

APPLY
My Role Is...?
Groups of 4–5 complete **Activity Sheet 74**.
- Students read *Investigate*.
- Then, students complete the concept map for *Apply*.
- Distribute copies of the **Journal (p. W3)** for students to respond to *Analyze*.

Possible Answers APPLY Answers to mind map will vary but might include: researcher, writer, artist or graphic designer, technology expert, speaker. Answers to **ANALYZE** will vary, based on personal skills and experience.

☐ CLASS WORK ☐ HOMEWORK
☐ EXTRA CREDIT ☐ PROJECT

EXTEND
Connect to Business Literacy
All successful businesses make money through teamwork. Many different people contribute to the business.

Think about a local business you visit often—perhaps a café, a store, or a restaurant. Make a collage of people who represent the roles of each person who makes that business a success. Find the images online or in **magazines**. Below each image, write responsibilities of the role. Present your collage as an electronic slideshow or as a **poster**.

☐ CLASS WORK ☐ HOMEWORK
☐ EXTRA CREDIT ☐ PROJECT

Unit 1 Life Skills

NAME _____ DATE _____

My Role Is...?

INVESTIGATE Create roles and responsibilities for a group project.

Work with a group on a project about volcanoes. The project has to be well researched. The typed research report must be presented aloud to the class using visual aids and notes in an electronic slideshow. Think about the different roles people will have in this project. What responsibilities and skills are needed for each role?

APPLY In the concept map below, fill in the roles, responsibilities, and skills required for each role in each box.

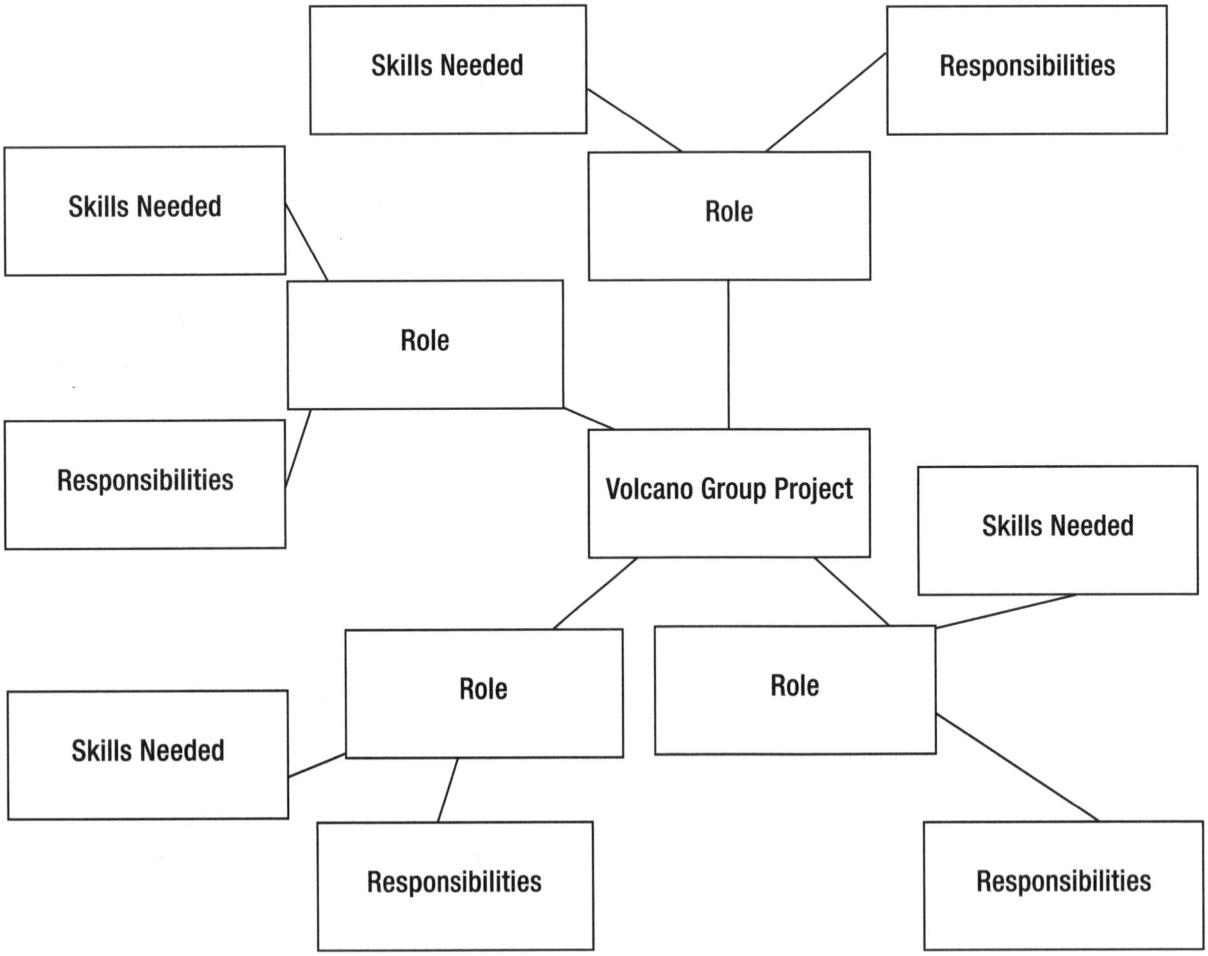

[Concept map with central box "Volcano Group Project" connected to four "Role" boxes, each connected to "Skills Needed" and "Responsibilities" boxes.]

ANALYZE Answer these questions in your Journal.

1. If you had to choose any of the roles from your mind map above, which would it be? Why?
2. What skills do you have that would make you able to do the job well?

4   Lesson 74 Defining Roles and Responsibilities   © 2011 Saddleback Educational Publishing

74 WHY TRY? Because— I'm part of a team!

Dealing with Change

75

DEALING WITH CHANGE

INTRODUCE THINK ABOUT IT *What changes have you had to deal with in your life? How did you handle those changes?*

TEACH LISTEN UP! We all deal with change sometimes. Change can come at school, home, work, or even in our relationships with others.
- Change sometimes causes strong feelings or **stress**.
- It's important to keep a **positive attitude** about change.
- A **negative attitude** can make it harder to deal with change.
- Change often requires rethinking a set plan and taking **action**.

Discuss some things that make students "stressed out," such as when a school project is due, studying for a test, arguments at home, or with trouble with friends. Ask: *What are some positive ways you deal with the stress?*

LET'S EXPLORE As a class, develop lists of responses to the following scenario: *You are working on a group project. The team member in charge of making the digital slideshow gets sick, so now you have to do it. You have never done this before and do not know how.*
- Create a 4-column chart on the board with these headings: Feelings About the Change, Positive Responses, Negative Responses, Actions to Take.
- Call on students for ideas for each heading, and discuss the ideas.

PLAY THESE ROLES A father tells his daughter that he just got a new job, and their family must move to a new place across the country.

▶ *Is the daughter's response positive or negative?*
negative, if she yells and is angry; positive, if she sees it as a chance to meet new people

▶ *Did the father help reduce or increase the stress on her?*
Reduce: He is understanding of her feelings. Increase: He is angry at her response.

REFLECT *How can you use change to grow in new ways?*

LESSON OBJECTIVE
Work effectively in a climate of ambiguity and changing priorities.

TERMS TO KNOW
action: the steps you take to achieve a goal
negative attitude: the act of looking at a situation in a bad way
positive attitude: the act of looking at a situation in a good way
stress: the state of feeling nervous and upset about something

GOES WELL WITH LESSONS: 10, 69, 74

21st Century Activities ... Each done in under **21** minutes

PRACTICE
Take Action!
Small groups generate positive responses and actions for a change scenario.
- Write change scenarios on **Note Cards (p. W10)**. Include examples from *Listen Up!* or others, such as starting a new job, joining a new team, or learning a new skill. Give one card to each group.
- The group acts out the scenario, focusing on a positive response.
- Then the rest of the class identifies additional actions that could be taken to deal with the change.

☐ CLASS WORK   ☐ HOMEWORK
☐ EXTRA CREDIT   ☐ PROJECT

APPLY
Stress Busters!
Individuals complete **Activity Sheet 75**.
- Students read, and then respond to *Analyze*.
- For *Create*, distribute the **Journal (p. W3)**. Provide **computer lab time** for online image searches and word processing, if available. Also provide **magazines** or **art supplies** for students to choose hard copy images or create their own.

Possible Answers Answers to *ANALYZE* and *CREATE* will vary, depending on personal experience.

☐ CLASS WORK   ☐ HOMEWORK
☐ EXTRA CREDIT   ☐ PROJECT

EXTEND
Connect to Health Literacy
Change often causes stress in people's lives. Stress, if not dealt with, can harm the body and mind.

Do some brief Internet research on the effects of stress on the body and mind. Then, choose one effect to use in an anti-stress advertisement. In your ad, include an image (electronic, hard-copy, or hand-drawn). Also include words to explain why people need to reduce their stress. Make your ad with a **computer program** or on **poster board**.

☐ CLASS WORK   ☐ HOMEWORK
☐ EXTRA CREDIT   ☐ PROJECT

Unit 1 Life Skills   5

NAME _____ DATE _____

Stress Busters!

75 WHY TRY? Because— Change can be good!

INVESTIGATE Read about some ways to handle stress.

The following dos and don'ts might help you deal with stress in a positive way.
- Don't blame others for your problems. Instead, look for solutions to the problems.
- Do avoid having a "poor-me" attitude.
- Don't try to be perfect. Quit trying to see "what's wrong." Focus on "what's right."
- Don't worry about things you can't control. Don't fill your mind with negative "what ifs."

Sometimes you may still feel "stressed out." If that happens, try some of these stress busters:
- Yell into or pound on pillows to let your feelings out. Emotions are energy that need to be released.
- Exercise. Some people think that exercise releases a body chemical that helps you to feel happier.
- Take deep breaths. Deep breaths bring more oxygen into your body. This helps you to relax. It also gives you more energy.
- Get plenty of sleep and eat a healthy diet. A healthy body is better able to handle stress.
- Talk to others. Discuss the problems in your life with those who care and can help. Opening up can make you feel better.
- Forgive yourself and others for making mistakes.

ANALYZE Think about what you read. Then, answer the questions below.

1. Underline ideas in the list above that you have already used to fight stress. Circle ideas you haven't tried but would like to. Which ideas do you feel might work the best for you? Why?

_____

2. What ways other than the ideas on the list above do you use to fight stress? What activities make you feel relaxed?

_____

CREATE Create a list of your own stress busters.

3. In your **Journal** make a list for yourself of ways you can fight stress every day. You can use ideas from the list above, but you should also include some of your own ways to relax, such as listening to a particular type of music. Draw or find an image that reminds you not to worry so much. Then, tape the list to the inside of your locker or put it in a good place at home. Look at the list when you feel stressed.

Lesson 75 Dealing with Change © 2011 Saddleback Educational Publishing

Accepting and Giving Feedback

76

INTRODUCE **THINK ABOUT IT** *Think of a time you gave feedback to someone. Did the person accept the feedback well? Were you comfortable giving feedback? Explain.*

TEACH **LISTEN UP!** We give **feedback** in order to help other people improve their work or behavior. For example, a teacher may tell you that an assignment you did needs more work. Or a coach may point out mistakes you are making. We accept feedback in order to improve our own work or behavior. To make the most out of feedback, follow these guidelines.

- **Give Constructive Criticism** Consider people's feelings. Choose words carefully.
- **Start with Strengths** Begin by praising things the person did well. Then constructively criticize things that need improvement.
- **Be Specific** Explain the work or behavior that needs improving and ways to improve.
- **Stay Positive** Be calm and focused when you give or accept feedback. See feedback as an opportunity to improve, not as a personal attack.

LET'S EXPLORE As a class, brainstorm situations in which people give and accept feedback.
- Think of situations. They could be at home or work, in school, or with friends.
- Write the ideas on the board. The class then votes to choose one situation to discuss.
- Ask: *In this situation, what should we say or do to give feedback? To accept it?*

PLAY THESE ROLES Students form pairs or small groups to role-play the situation they just discussed. Each student takes a role and uses the guidelines for accepting and giving feedback. Observe role-plays; if necessary, model how to give and get constructive criticism.

REFLECT *What have you learned about feedback? How, specifically, can you use what you learned?*

ACCEPTING AND GIVING FEEDBACK

LESSON OBJECTIVE
Use feedback to improve work and respond effectively to praise, setbacks, and criticism.

TERMS TO KNOW
constructive criticism: useful advice given with regard for a person's feelings to help the person improve
feedback: evaluation of a person's work or behavior

GOES WELL WITH LESSONS:
20, 54, 107

21st Century Activities ... Each done in under 21 minutes

PRACTICE
Peer Feedback
Partners offer feedback to each other on writing assignments.
- Students select a writing assignment they are working on or have completed.
- Pairs exchange assignments and write feedback notes on another sheet of paper.
- Students use the guidelines and their notes to give and accept feedback.
- Listen and observe to assess students' understanding.
- Give feedback to pairs.

☐ CLASS WORK ☐ HOMEWORK
☐ EXTRA CREDIT ☐ PROJECT

APPLY
Receiving Feedback
Individuals complete **Activity Sheet 76**.
- Students read the story.
- Students respond to the questions; the class discusses.

Possible Answers 1. "You and your staff usually do a great job. But, on Saturday I received two complaints."
2. Yes, she said what happened, when it happened, and how many customers were involved. **EVALUATE:** Yes, he followed all the guidelines, and he got his salespeople involved in coming up with solutions. Ms. Hernandez was pleased.

☐ CLASS WORK ☐ HOMEWORK
☐ EXTRA CREDIT ☐ PROJECT

EXTEND
Connect to Civic Literacy
City governments must balance the needs of different groups of people—senior citizens, adults, teenagers, and children to name a few. How well do you think our city meets the needs of area teenagers? Is there something the city could do better?

Write an e-mail that you could send to the mayor or other city leaders. Be sure to follow the guidelines for giving feedback.

☐ CLASS WORK ☐ HOMEWORK
☐ EXTRA CREDIT ☐ PROJECT

Unit 1 Life Skills 7

NAME _____ DATE _____

Evaluate Feedback

76 WHY TRY? Because— Feedback can help me improve!

INVESTIGATE Read the story "Chris and Ms. Hernandez." As you read, underline times when the people followed the feedback guidelines below.

- **Give Constructive Criticism** Consider people's feelings. Choose words carefully.
- **Start with Strengths** Praise strengths first; then point out areas for improvement.
- **Be Specific** Explain what work or behavior needs improving and how to improve.
- **Stay Positive** Be calm and focused when you give or accept feedback.

Chris and Ms. Hernandez

Chris runs the shoe department of a large store. One day, Ms. Hernandez, the store manager, calls him to her office. She says, "Chris, you know we pride ourselves on giving good service. You and your staff usually do a great job. But, on Saturday I received two complaints. Two customers were unhappy with the shoe department. Both said the staff ignored them. One customer said she told you, but you didn't seem to care. I think I know you better than that. But somehow you made the customer feel that way."

Chris is embarrassed, but he stays calm and focused. He thanks Ms. Hernandez and says he will take care of the problem. That afternoon, he talks to his salespeople. He tells them what Ms. Hernandez said. Then he says, "I know how hard you work, and I know how busy we were Saturday. I also know you have great ideas. How can we solve the problem of customers' feeling ignored?" The salespeople discuss what happened Saturday. They give good solutions. Chris meets again with Ms. Hernandez to explain his salespeople's plan. He asks her for feedback. She smiles and says, "Sounds good. Let's try it!"

UNDERSTAND Think about what you read. Then answer the questions.

1. Give an example of a time when Ms. Hernandez gave constructive criticism.

_____

2. Did Ms. Hernandez give specific feedback? Explain.

_____

EVALUATE Think about Chris's response to Ms. Hernandez's feedback. Was it effective? Explain why or why not.

_____

Lesson 76 Accepting and Giving Feedback © 2011 Saddleback Educational Publishing

Resolving Conflicts at Home and in School

RESOLVING CONFLICTS AT HOME AND IN SCHOOL

INTRODUCE **THINK ABOUT IT** *What kinds of conflicts have you had with friends? How did you resolve the conflicts?*

TEACH **LISTEN UP!** People do not always see eye to eye. Sometimes, you disagree with others at home or in school. To resolve everyday conflicts, remember these guidelines:
- **Stay Calm** Don't let strong feelings keep you from thinking clearly.
- **Try to See Other People's Point of View** Listen to what the other person or people have to say. Try to figure out how they feel and why. See things from their viewpoints.
- **Find a Common Goal** If you are a member of a work group whose members disagree, for example, remind everyone that they have the same aim: to do good work on time.
- **Compromise, or Take Positive Actions** Stay positive. Think of ways to end the conflict without lasting negative effects. Be willing to give up a little to resolve the conflict.
- **Ask an Adult for Help** If necessary, ask an adult to step in to help or to give advice.

LET'S EXPLORE Give students this scenario: *One member of a work group does not do her share. She says she's too busy. Her actions have caused conflict within the group.*
- On the board, write these headings: Positive Responses, Negative Responses.
- Students use the guidelines to suggest how to end the conflict. List suggestions.
- Students vote to find the three best ways to resolve the conflict.

PLAY THESE ROLES Give students this scenario: *A parent tells his or her teenager that he or she must babysit for a younger brother or sister and therefore cannot go out with friends. This causes conflict between the parent and teen.* Have partners select roles and use the guidelines to resolve the conflict. Observe role-plays and offer suggestions.

REFLECT *Which conflict-resolution guidelines would you most like to try, and why?*

LESSON OBJECTIVE
Understand, negotiate, and balance diverse views and beliefs to reach workable solutions.

TERMS TO KNOW
compromise: an agreement in which both sides give up something they want in order resolve a conflict
conflict: a disagreement or misunderstanding
positive actions: the steps taken to end a conflict in a way that balances differing viewpoints
resolve: to end or settle

GOES WELL WITH LESSONS: 21, 55, 95

21st Century Activities ... Each done in under **21** minutes

PRACTICE
Resolve This Conflict
Present this conflict: *A father tells his daughter she must do her chores. The daughter refuses.*
- Half the class sees the conflict from the father's viewpoint; the other half, from the daughter's.
- Each group brainstorms reasons why his or her viewpoint is right, then presents the reasons to the class.
- The two groups then "talk out" the conflict, offering ways to reach a compromise. You act as a mediator / facilitator.

☐ CLASS WORK ☐ HOMEWORK
☐ EXTRA CREDIT ☐ PROJECT

APPLY
Let's Work It Out!
Pairs complete **Activity Sheet 77.**
- Partners read the story and complete the chart.
- Partners answer the question.

Possible Answers Stay Calm: Think, rather than react. **Try to See Other People's Points of View:** Ask the friends why they don't like Rashad. **Find a Common Goal:** Point out you could all have fun together. **Compromise, or Take Positive Actions:** Go out with friends without Rashad another time. **Ask an Adult for Help:** Ask for advice. **SELECT:** Answers will vary.

☐ CLASS WORK ☐ HOMEWORK
☐ EXTRA CREDIT ☐ PROJECT

EXTEND
Connect to Health Literacy
Imagine that a younger brother or sister spends all of his or her free time in front of the TV and the computer. Time and again, you've pointed out the need for fresh air and exercise, but this has only made your sibling feel angry and picked on. You, in turn, are upset with your sibling.

Choose two of the conflict-resolution guidelines. Describe how you would use them to resolve the conflict. Present your ideas to the class.

☐ CLASS WORK ☐ HOMEWORK
☐ EXTRA CREDIT ☐ PROJECT

Unit 1 Life Skills

NAME _____ DATE _____

Let's Work It Out!

77 WHY TRY? Because— Ending conflicts helps everyone!

INVESTIGATE Read the story below about a conflict between friends.

A Conflict Among Friends

Rashad is a new student at school. He doesn't have any friends yet, but he seems nice. You invite Rashad to eat lunch with you and your friends so he doesn't have to sit alone. At first, your friends ignore him. Then they begin to say unkind things to him at lunch. When you ask your friends to stop, they make fun of you. The conflict grows when you invite Rashad to a party you're having. Your best friend says, "Why did you invite him? Nobody but you likes him. If he's going, the rest of us are staying home."

APPLY Explain how you could use each guideline to help resolve the conflict.

Stay Calm:
Try to See Other People's Points of View:
Find a Common Goal:
Compromise, or Take Positive Actions:
Ask an Adult for Help:

SELECT From the chart, choose two ways that you think would best resolve the conflict. Explain why you chose these ways.

_____

_____

Lesson 77 Resolving Conflicts at Home and in School © 2011 Saddleback Educational Publishing

Setting and Meeting Goals

78

SETTING AND MEETING GOALS

INTRODUCE **THINK ABOUT IT** *Have you ever wanted to accomplish something but were not sure how to go about it? Did it need to be done soon or far in the future?*

TEACH **LISTEN UP!** Setting and meeting goals is a challenge for everyone, especially those inexperienced at it. It's helpful to understand these three types of related goals.

1. **Long-term goals** are far in the future and take many steps to achieve.
2. **Mid-term goals** are steps you take to help get to the long-term goal.
3. **Short-term goals** are smaller steps to the mid-term goal.

Tell students that it's a good idea to break up goals into manageable steps. Here's how:
- Break the goal into small, manageable parts or steps.
- Divide up the time you have left by setting a deadline for each step.
- Check off the steps as you meet each one.

LET'S EXPLORE As a class, develop a list of goals that students have or want to have.
- As students state their goals, ask them to identify which type of goal it is.
- Write the goals on the board under the heading *long-term, mid-term,* or *short-term.*
- Choose a short-term goal to break into steps. Divide the time and assign deadlines
  Example: The steps to write a report are research, outline, draft, revise, finalize.

TIME FOR Q & A Discover how the different types of goals are connected. Select a few interesting long-term goals from the list you created in *Let's Explore* for Q & A.

▸ **What is a mid-term goal that can help us meet this long-term goal?**
  Example: Erin's long-term goal is to be a teacher. A good mid-term goal would be to earn her college degree.

▸ **What are some short-term goals related to this mid-term one?**
  Example: Erin's short-term goals might be to ace her final exams and find a part-time job working with kids.

REFLECT *How can you set goals that you know you can meet?*

LESSON OBJECTIVE
Set and meet long-term, mid-term, and short-term goals.

TERMS TO KNOW
long-term goals: aims that are far in the future and take many steps to achieve
mid-term goals: steps you take to help reach a long-term goal
short-term goals: tasks or steps that needs to be accomplished in the very near future

GOES WELL WITH LESSONS: 35, 71, 80

21st Century Activities ... Each done in under **21** minutes

PRACTICE
Make a Short-Term Plan
Small groups plan how to meet a short-term goal in 1–2 weeks.
- Choose a short-term goal common to the group or from the class list.
- Break up the goal into three or more basic steps.
- Assign deadlines for each step on a **calendar.**
- Present the plan to the class if time allows.

Goal ideas: clean your room or locker; organize a closet or bookshelf; study for an exam; practice for a try-out or audition; complete a class project

☐ CLASS WORK   ☐ HOMEWORK
☐ EXTRA CREDIT ☐ PROJECT

APPLY
Set Your Goals
Individuals complete **Activity Sheet 78.**
- Read investigate.
- Complete the goal pyramid for items 1–3 in *Evaluate.*
- Responses to *Synthesize* can appear on a separate sheet of paper or in **journals.**

Possible Answers 1. Answers will vary but goal should be at least a year in the future. **2.** Answers will vary but goal should be a step toward first goal. **3.** Goal should be near term and related to goals 2 and 1.
SYNTHESIZE: Answers will vary.

☐ CLASS WORK   ☐ HOMEWORK
☐ EXTRA CREDIT ☐ PROJECT

EXTEND
Connecting to Economic Literacy
Sometimes you need to set goals related to personal economic choices. For example, you may want a dress for the prom but need to earn the money yourself.

Think about a goal you have that requires you to save or spend money. Make a plan for how you can make the money and reach your goal. Present the plan using a **spreadsheet** or on **graph paper.**

☐ CLASS WORK   ☐ HOMEWORK
☐ EXTRA CREDIT ☐ PROJECT

Unit 1 Life Skills   11

NAME _____ DATE _____

Set Your Goals

WHY TRY? Because— I can set and reach my goals!

INVESTIGATE Your goals are aims you hope to achieve.

- **Long-term goals** are aims for the long-term future.
- **Mid-term goals** are aims that will lead to the target—the long-term goal.
- **Short-term goals** are small steps that you can complete in a fairly short period of time.

LONG-TERM
Graduate from high school.

MID-TERM
Pass U.S. history, world history, and American government.

SHORT-TERM
Complete U.S. history project, study for final test, and sign up for next term's American government class.

A goal pyramid like the one shown can help you picture these goals.

EVALUATE Make your own goal pyramid. Write the answer to each question on the line that matches the number.

1. What is a long-term goal you would like to accomplish in the next ten years?

2. What are some mid-term goals you must accomplish in the next two years to reach your ten-year goal?

3. What are some short-term goals you must accomplish in the next six months to reach your two-year goal?

1. _____

2. _____

3. _____

SYNTHESIZE Think of a goal you would like to reach in one month. In your journals, make a pyramid. Show the long-term goal (one month), plus mid-term (two week) and short-term (daily) steps toward the goal. For example, your pyramid might list steps that would lead to passing an important math test, improving your physical fitness, or writing your own blog.

Lesson 78 Setting and Meeting Goals © 2011 Saddleback Educational Publishing

Asking for Help

79

ASKING FOR HELP

INTRODUCE THINK ABOUT IT *When do you know it is time to ask someone for help? How do you go about asking?*

TEACH LISTEN UP! We all need to ask for help sometimes—at school, at home, at work, and even in our relationships with others. Asking for help is important when things are unclear, or when **priorities** change. Follow these steps when deciding if it is time to ask for help.

1. **Monitor** the situation over time, if possible.
2. Stay calm. Figure out what needs to be done.
3. Decide what you can do to solve the problem.
4. If you are unable to fix the problem on your own, if things are unclear, or if priorities change, you should ask for help.

Remember: When asking for help, clearly and calmly explain the situation to someone. Then, ask for help politely.

LET'S EXPLORE Brainstorm for scenarios that might require asking for help.
- Create a **3-Column Chart (p. W5)** on the board with these headings: Home, School, Work.
- Call on students for scenarios that fall into each category. Remind them to explain what is unclear in each scenario, or what priorities have changed.
- Choose one scenario from each category and discuss who to ask for help in that scenario.

PLAY THESE ROLES A customer angrily approaches a store or restaurant worker with a complaint.

▶ *Did the worker first try to solve the problem herself? How?*
Yes, she calmly listened to the customer and tried to address his problem.

▶ *How did the worker know when it was time to ask for help?*
When the customer would not calm down, the worker knew she needed to call her manager.

REFLECT *Why is it important to ask for help when you need it?*

LESSON OBJECTIVE
Work to resolve problems involving ambiguity or changing priorities.

TERMS TO KNOW
monitor: to watch closely, often by recording information
priorities: the order or importance of things

GOES WELL WITH LESSONS:
21, 64, 98

21st Century Activities ... Each done in under **21** minutes

PRACTICE
Ask for Help!
Three groups work through scenarios using the steps in *Listen Up!*.
- Assign each group one scenario:
  1. a big argument with a friend or family member;
  2. needing ideas for a group project;
  3. using a new computer program at work.
- Each group generates ideas on how to fix the problem on their own. Then, they generate ideas for people they could ask for help and discuss how they would ask.

Each group presents its ideas to the class. If time allows, role-play.

☐ CLASS WORK ☐ HOMEWORK
☐ EXTRA CREDIT ☐ PROJECT

APPLY
Monitor Your Work
Individuals complete **Activity Sheet 79**.
- Students review their graded work for one week and complete the chart. Then, they answer the *Evaluate* questions.
- Distribute **Spreadsheet (p. W12)** for students to complete and monitor future progress and identify when to ask for help.

Possible Answers 1. Social Studies. I didn't do well on the tests. **2.** My teacher. I could ask her to clarify what chapters are most important to study. **CREATE** Answers will vary.

☐ CLASS WORK ☐ HOMEWORK
☐ EXTRA CREDIT ☐ PROJECT

EXTEND
Connect to Health Literacy
Questions about health arise in everyone's life. That's why we ask doctors for help.

Do brief online research about a health-related topic, such as nutrition, exercise, stress reduction, hygiene, and so on. Create an "Ask Your Doctor About…" poster, either on **poster board** or using a **computer program**. Be sure to include information about why asking your doctor about that particular topic is important and how to ask. Also include an image or images on the poster.

☐ CLASS WORK ☐ HOMEWORK
☐ EXTRA CREDIT ☐ PROJECT

Unit 1 Life Skills

NAME _____ DATE _____

Monitor Your Work

79 WHY TRY? Because— Everyone needs help sometimes!

INVESTIGATE Use the chart below to monitor your school work for the past week.

Monitoring your work helps you to know when it is time to ask for help. Add other subject areas, if necessary, to the far left column. Add the dates in the top row. In the other boxes, add the type of work and the grade you got on it. Use these labels for the type of work:
H = homework; Q = quiz; T = test; P = project.

	Date	Date	Date	Date	Date
Math					
Reading					
Science					
Social Studies					

EVALUATE Review the grades you recorded in the chart. Then, answer these questions.

1. Which subject area shows the lowest grades? What might the reason be?

_____

2. Who could you ask for help in raising your grades? What could you say to that person when asking for help?

_____

CREATE Using your Spreadsheet, make a chart like the one above to help you monitor your school work for a month. Add in each grade you get for the next month. Carefully monitor your progress. If you see that you are struggling in a certain subject, try to figure out what the problem is. Ask for help with that problem from a teacher, classmate, or parent/guardian.

Lesson 79 Asking for Help © 2011 Saddleback Educational Publishing

Following Schedules

INTRODUCE **THINK ABOUT IT** *Have you ever followed a schedule in order to get something done?*

TEACH **LISTEN UP!** Ask students to think about the class **schedules** they get at the start of a school year. Point out that their schedules are **organized** by the school. Explain that anyone can set and follow a schedule in order to organize their time and complete **tasks**. Write the following questions on the board to get students thinking about how to set a schedule.
- What needs to be done?
- How long will it take?
- When is it due?

LET'S EXPLORE Brainstorm a list of situations in which a schedule would be helpful for organizing time or tasks. Student ideas may include a schedule for practicing a musical instrument, sharing cleaning responsibilities, or working a part-time job.
- As a class, spend 3–5 minutes brainstorming.
- Write all student ideas on the board.
- Encourage ideas by asking: *When have you relied on a schedule?*

THINK, PAIR, SHARE Have students work with a partner to discuss how they have followed a schedule to achieve a goal or complete a task. Tell students to think about a time they followed a schedule. Ask students to describe the situation to their partner, and explain how following a schedule helped them to organize their time.

REFLECT *How can following a schedule help you achieve a goal?*

80

FOLLOWING SCHEDULES

LESSON OBJECTIVE
Create and follow a schedule.

TERMS TO KNOW
organized: arranged; put in order
schedules: plans of things to be done in a set amount of time
tasks: jobs, chores, things to be done

GOES WELL WITH LESSONS:
4, 41, 89

21st Century Activities ... Each done in under 21 minutes

PRACTICE
All in a Day
Guide students in building a schedule for a day of events.
- Have students share examples of events from daily life, such as attending sports practice, taking care of siblings, or working a part-time job.
- Ask students to write their examples on the board.
- Discuss how best to organize the events in order to set a schedule.
- Point out that while this is an imaginary schedule, students can use the same process to build individual schedules for themselves.

☐ CLASS WORK   ☐ HOMEWORK
☐ EXTRA CREDIT   ☐ PROJECT

APPLY
Team Clean
Individuals complete **Activity Sheet 80**.
- Study the sample schedule.
- For *Apply*, brainstorm possible household cleaning tasks that need to be completed in one week.
- Create a weekly cleaning schedule using the **Planner (p. W11)**.

Possible Answers for *APPLY* and *DESIGN* will vary, but should reflect understanding of a realistic schedule.

☐ CLASS WORK   ☐ HOMEWORK
☐ EXTRA CREDIT   ☐ PROJECT

EXTEND
Connect to Business Literacy
Television stations need a schedule to communicate with consumers. Without the television listings, no one would know when their favorite show aired!

Write a list of television shows that you enjoy watching each week. Include the days and times they are on television. Then write a list of other forms of entertainment you do each week, such as go to the movies, play video games, chat on the Web, and so on. Create an entertainment schedule for yourself, using a chart like one on the activity sheet or in an electronic spreadsheet.

☐ CLASS WORK   ☐ HOMEWORK
☐ EXTRA CREDIT   ☐ PROJECT

Unit 1 Life Skills   15

NAME _____ DATE _____

Team Clean

80 WHY TRY? Because— Schedules help to get jobs done!

INVESTIGATE Following a schedule can help you complete a job or achieve a goal. Read the sample schedule below.

JOB	PAT	CHRIS	JUSTIN	DO YOUR OWN
Empty garbage	Mon., Tues.	Wed., Thurs.	Fri., Sat., Sun.	
Make bed				daily
Load dishwasher				daily (rinse and load your own dishes)
Empty dishwasher	Mon., Tues.	Wed., Thurs.	Fri., Sat., Sun,	
Clean toilet and bathroom	Mon., Tues.	Wed., Thurs.	Fri., Sat., Sun	
Wipe shower stall				daily
clean kitchen counters, sink				daily (as you use them)
Feed cats; clean up after them	Mon., Tues.	Wed., Thurs.	Fri., Sat., Sun.	
Clean out cat litter box	Mon., Tues	Wed., Thurs.	Fri., Sat., Sun.	
Vacuum common living areas	Sat.			
Dust common living areas		Sat.		
Water plants in common areas			Sat.	
Do laundry				weekly
Sweep kitchen floor	Mon., Tues.	Wed., Thurs.	Fri., Sat., Sun.	
Wash kitchen floor	Sat.			
Clean bedroom (vacuum, dust, change sheets)				weekly

APPLY You will set a schedule for your family to share the cleaning jobs. Make a list of jobs you will write on the schedule. For this exercise, focus on one week of jobs. Your ideas might include:

- dusting furniture
- vacuuming a room
- watering plants
- washing the dishes

You may also use ideas from the chart above or come up with your own jobs.

DESIGN Use the Planner to plan your schedule for a day of cleaning jobs. Write the tasks outside the left column. Place the names across the top. Assign each person a task to complete.

16   Lesson 80 Following Schedules   © 2011 Saddleback Educational Publishing

Following a Budget

81

INTRODUCE THINK ABOUT IT *When you want to buy something new, how do you make decisions about how much money to spend?*

FOLLOWING A BUDGET

TEACH LISTEN UP! It's easy to spend money. It's harder to keep track of spending. That's why it's important to keep good **financial** records and to follow a **budget.** Following a budget helps you track your spending, save money, and avoid **debt.** A budget includes two things:
- **Income** includes the amount of money you expect to earn.
- **Expenses** include the amount of money you expect to spend.

LET'S EXPLORE Brainstorm a list of common and necessary expenses.
- Ask: *What are some common expenses a family spends money on?*
- Write student ideas on the board. The list may include rent, groceries, and utilities such as gas and electric bills.
- Point out that a budget helps to plan for spending money on necessary expenses, such as food and housing, before unnecessary expenses, such as new clothes or jewelry.

TIME FOR Q & A Discover more about planning and following a budget.

▸ *How can receipts help you follow a budget?*
Recording receipts helps you track expenses.

▸ *What happens if you spend more than your income?*
You will go into debt.

▸ *How do you know how much you can spend each month?*
Your income shows you how much money you have available.

▸ *When can you spend money on the things you want?*
after you have budgeted money for the things you need

LESSON OBJECTIVE
Plan and follow a budget.

TERMS TO KNOW
budget: a written spending plan
financial: anything having to do with money
debt: money you owe

GOES WELL WITH LESSONS:
15, 71, 106

REFLECT *How can following a budget help you make good financial decisions?*

21st Century Activities ... Each done in under 21 minutes

PRACTICE
Buy Now
Practice making financial decisions.
- Give each student $100 in **play money.**
- Tell students they have 5 minutes to decide how they will spend this money. Have them list their expenses.
- After five minutes, ask volunteers to share their list of expenses with the class. Discuss whether each expense is a need or a want.
- Ask students if anyone set some of their play money aside for savings.

☐ CLASS WORK ☐ HOMEWORK
☐ EXTRA CREDIT ☐ PROJECT

APPLY
Budget It!
Small groups complete **Activity Sheet 81.**
- Read through the sample family budget with students.
- Tell groups to calculate the monthly expenses and the amount left over.
- Students work together to decide how to budget the remainder of the monthly income.

Possible Answers APPLY:
Expenses: $830. Remaining: $970.
CREATE: Answers will vary, but should show an amount for savings and items and amounts for "Wants."

☐ CLASS WORK ☐ HOMEWORK
☐ EXTRA CREDIT ☐ PROJECT

EXTEND
Connect to Financial Literacy
Consider the taxes we pay on goods and services. A budget must be based on items' prices after taxes are taken into consideration.

Tell students what the sales tax is in your county. Briefly model how to calculate sales tax on an item. Have students create a chart using a **Spreadsheet (p. W12)** that shows the total cost of purchasing the following items both before and after taxes: CD, $17; basketball, $15.80; candy bar, $1.25; DVD, $14.99; tennis shoes, $65.

☐ CLASS WORK ☐ HOMEWORK
☐ EXTRA CREDIT ☐ PROJECT

Unit 1 Life Skills

NAME _____ DATE _____

Budget It!

INVESTIGATE Read the sample budget below to find out how this family plans for necessary expenses every month.

81 WHY TRY? Because— It's important to use money wisely!

MONTHLY BUDGET _____

Income		$1800.00
Expenses (Needs)	Rent	$500.00
	Car Payment	$125.00
	Car Insurance	$60.00
	Phone	$100.00
	Electric	$45.00
	Savings	$50.00

TOTAL NEEDS EXPENSES: _____

BALANCE (subtract from income): _____

Expenses (Wants) _____   _____

_____   _____

_____   _____

TOTAL WANTS EXPENSES: _____

NEW BALANCE (subtract from previous balance): _____

APPLY Add up the total amount of monthly expenses for needs. Then subtract that amount from the monthly income. Enter these amounts in the chart. The Balance is the amount of money the family can use in other ways.

CREATE Plan the rest of the family's budget. Decide how much the family can save each month. Discuss other "Wants" expenses with your group. Show how much will be spent on the things the family wants. Your ideas might include:

- going out to the movies
- going out to dinner
- clothing
- electronics
- books and magazines

Fill in the chart to complete the monthly budget.

18 Lesson 81 Following a Budget   © 2011 Saddleback Educational Publishing

Furthering Your Education

INTRODUCE THINK ABOUT IT *Do you know what different kinds of schools you might choose from after you finish high school? Colleges are one kind. What are some others?*

TEACH LISTEN UP! Point out that about 70 percent of high-school graduates further their education after high school. Among the options that may be open to students are these:

- **Community colleges,** or local colleges where students can earn a 2- or 4-year degree.
- **Vocational schools,** where students can learn trades such as plumbing or hairdressing.
- **Universities,** where students can earn 4-year degrees, master's degrees, and Ph.Ds.
- **Online colleges,** where students can earn degrees by taking classes over the Internet.

LET'S EXPLORE Name as many post-secondary schools as possible.
- Ask volunteers to name post-secondary schools they know.
- List students' ideas on the board or on chart paper.
- Review the list and determine what category each school fits.
- Ask students to name various jobs and careers. Help students determine what type of school or schools they might attend for each career.

REVERSE Q & A Have students pose questions they have about post-secondary education.

▸ *How can you find information about schools you might go to?*
Internet searches and talks with school counselors are two ways to start.

▸ *Isn't school too expensive?*
Most schools offer financial aid, and you may be able to take out loans.

▸ *How can you find out how much education you need for a career?*
One way is to look in the *Occupational Outlook Handbook.*

▸ *Do I need a high GPA?*
not at **open-admissions** schools

REFLECT *How can thinking about career goals help you decide what type of education to get?*

82

FURTHERING YOUR EDUCATION

LESSON OBJECTIVE
Distinguish between kinds of post-secondary schools and write a sample college-application response.

TERMS TO KNOW
GPA: grade-point average, calculated by dividing grade points earned by number of credits attempted
open admissions: a policy that allows anyone with a high school diploma to enroll

GOES WELL WITH LESSONS:
23, 44, 73

21st Century Activities ... Each done in under 21 minutes

PRACTICE
School Wish List
Students answer questions to think about what they want in a school.
- Give students school-related questions to answer, such as:
- *What job or career might you want?*
- *Would you prefer a small school or a big one?*
- *Would you like to live at home, near home, or far from home?*
- *Does a sports program matter to you? Do other activities?*
- Encourage students to use their answers to research schools.

☐ CLASS WORK ☐ HOMEWORK
☐ EXTRA CREDIT ☐ PROJECT

APPLY
Write to an Application Prompt
Individuals complete **Activity Sheet 82.**
- Read aloud the prompt and the student response.
- Students evaluate the response.
- Students write their responses to the prompt, then exchange responses and proofread.

Possible Answers EVALUATE: The student's response is good. It is focused, clear, well-organized, and well-supported.
WRITE: Responses should display the same characteristics as the sample.

☐ CLASS WORK ☐ HOMEWORK
☐ EXTRA CREDIT ☐ PROJECT

EXTEND
Connect to Financial Literacy
If you want to further your education after high school, you can usually find sources of money. Bank loans and government loans, school financial-aid packages, and scholarships are a few. First, you need to figure out what kinds of expenses you might have.

Brainstorm a list of things you might need to pay for, such as a place to stay if you go away to school. Compare your list with another group's. Make a master expense list.

☐ CLASS WORK ☐ HOMEWORK
☐ EXTRA CREDIT ☐ PROJECT

Unit 1 Life Skills   19

Write to an Application Prompt

INVESTIGATE To apply for colleges and other schools, you must fill out an application form. Many application forms ask you to write a short response to a prompt, or a topic. Read the example prompt. Then read a student's answer.

> PROMPT: In 100 words or less, tell us what strengths you would bring to our college.
>
> RESPONSE: I would bring leadership, dedication, and a sense of humor. I have shown leadership as captain of the junior varsity volleyball team. I was also co-captain of the varsity team. I have also always been a dedicated student. This year, I got the Outstanding Attendance Award. I have also always finished all assignments on time. Finally, I have a good sense of humor, and I love to laugh. Though I expect college to be stressful sometimes, I know a good sense of humor will help me cope.

82 WHY TRY? Because— An education will help me succeed!

EVALUATE Do you think the student did a good job of answering the question? Explain why or why not.

_____
_____
_____
_____

WRITE On the lines below, write your own response to the prompt. Then reread it to make sure you didn't make any mistakes. If you did, fix them.

_____
_____
_____
_____
_____
_____
_____
_____

Finding and Applying for a Job

INTRODUCE **THINK ABOUT IT** *Have you ever looked for a job? What steps did you take to find jobs for which you were qualified?*

TEACH **LISTEN UP!** At some time in their life, most people look for jobs in order to use the skills they have learned and earn money. Here are three sources you can look into for jobs:

- **Classified ads,** or newspaper listings of help-wanted advertisements
- **Online job databases,** or listings of help-wanted ads you can search over the Internet
- **State employment services,** or government-run services that help people find jobs

Whatever sources you use, look for jobs you are **qualified** for and interested in doing.

LET'S EXPLORE Model using classified ads to find and apply for a job.
- Provide students with pages from the jobs section of a local newspaper.
- Help students identify jobs that interest them as well as jobs for which they might be qualified now or later. Help students figure out the meanings of common job ad abbreviations, such as FT (full time), PT, (part time), and exp (experience).
- Tell students that when they apply for a job they will need to provide basic personal information, such as their name and address, as well as facts about the schools they have attended, diplomas or degrees they have earned, and jobs they have held.

REVERSE Q & A Students ask questions about how to find and apply for jobs.

▶ *Which is a better source of jobs: newspaper ads or online ads?*
Either is okay, but most employers are using online listings.

▶ *What is a résumé?*
a report listing a person's qualifications for a job, such as jobs and degrees held

▶ *What kinds of things can I find at State Employment Services?*
job listings and free help on how to apply for jobs, write résumés, etc.

▶ *How do I find online databases?*
Use key words, such as *jobs* and the name of your city or one nearby.

REFLECT *Which job sources do you plan to look into and why?*

83

FINDING AND APPLYING FOR A JOB

LESSON OBJECTIVE
Identify sources for finding jobs and complete a job application form.

TERMS TO KNOW
applicant: a person applying for a job
qualified: having the right experience or education for a particular job

GOES WELL WITH LESSONS:
22, 68, 84

21st Century Activities … Each done in under 21 minutes

PRACTICE
Your Time to Shine
Students discuss strengths and skills they might list when applying for jobs.
- Students think of things they know well, can do well, or naturally have, such as a good sense of humor.
- Students then think about the strengths and skills of each member in the group.
- Group members take turns telling each member strengths he or she possesses.

☐ CLASS WORK ☐ HOMEWORK
☐ EXTRA CREDIT ☐ PROJECT

APPLY
Complete a Job Application
Individuals complete **Activity Sheet 83.**
- Students read the application form.
- Students complete the form. (Allow students to keep their social security number private if they wish.)
- Students turn in the form, then evaluate each other's form.

Possible Answers Students' application forms will vary but should be complete, accurate, and error-free.

☐ CLASS WORK ☐ HOMEWORK
☐ EXTRA CREDIT ☐ PROJECT

EXTEND
Connect to Business Literacy
When interviewing for a job, it helps to have a "you attitude" and see things from the employer's point of view. For example, say, "You can count on me to be on time" rather than "I am always on time." Use these sentences-starters to practice "you attitude" sentences:
- The company might benefit from my. . .
- You can expect me to be. . .
- If you hire me, I will bring these skills to the job: . . .

☐ CLASS WORK ☐ HOMEWORK
☐ EXTRA CREDIT ☐ PROJECT

Unit 1 Life Skills

NAME _____ DATE _____

Complete a Job Application

83 WHY TRY? Because— I can get a good job!

INVESTIGATE ▶ Read the blank job application form.

Job Application Form

Company Name: _____

PERSONAL INFORMATION

Name _____
            LAST   FIRST   MIDDLE INITIAL

Address _____
          STREET   CITY

Telephone _____

Position You Are Applying For _____

EMPLOYMENT HISTORY — List two most recent jobs.

Company _____ **Address** _____

Supervisor _____ **Phone** _____

Dates Worked: From _____ **To** _____ **Reason for Leaving** _____

_____

Company _____ **Address** _____

Supervisor _____ **Phone** _____

Dates Worked: From _____ **To** _____ **Reason for Leaving** _____

_____

EDUCATION — List school most recently attended.

Name and Address _____

Last grade completed or degree earned _____

APPLY ▶ Think of a job you would like to apply for. Fill in the application form.

EVALUATE ▶ Exchange forms with a partner. Check each other's work. Fix any mistakes.

---

22   Lesson 83 Finding and Applying for a Job   © 2011 Saddleback Educational Publishing

Writing Résumés

84 WRITING RÉSUMÉS

INTRODUCE **THINK ABOUT IT** *Often, a job ad asks people to send their résumé to show they're qualified for a job. What is a résumé? Why is it important to have one?*

TEACH **LISTEN UP!** You don't have to have had paying jobs to write a **résumé.** Most people do not have job experience when they apply for their first job. Skills learned in school or through a hobby, volunteer work you have done, jobs you do at home or for neighbors—these things also can go on your résumé. To write a good résumé, follow these steps:

1. **Gather Information** List your skills, work experiences, and other qualifications. Include references you might use, such as people you've worked for or teachers.
2. **Organize Information** You can organize information on your résumé in different ways. Do an online search to find example résumés you like. Follow the examples.
3. **Write and Proofread** Write your résumé using a word processor if you can. Then proofread your résumé carefully. To make a good impression, it must be error-free.

LET'S EXPLORE Let's talk a little more about résumés and ways to send them.

- Three ways to send your résumé are by mail, by fax, or by e-mail. Check to see whether an employer prefers one way or another.
- If you send your résumé by mail, print it on good-quality white or off-white paper.
- If you post your résumé on a job **database,** avoid boldface, italics, or other formatting.

TIME FOR Q & A Let's see what else you know about résumés.

▶ **Why is it important to ask someone to be a reference before listing him or her?**
It's important to ask for permission from the reference, and also refresh his or her memory about your experience.

▶ **Can you use the same résumé for different jobs?**
Yes, but it helps to tailor it to a job.

LESSON OBJECTIVE
Write a résumé that could be used to apply for a job.

TERMS TO KNOW
database: a collection of information organized to make it easy to find specific facts
reference: a person qualified to recommend someone else for a job
résumé: a report that lists a person's qualifications for a job, such as jobs held, degrees earned, and accomplishments

GOES WELL WITH LESSONS:
18, 69, 83

REFLECT *What skills, experiences, or other qualifications could you list on your résumé?*

21st Century Activities ... Each done in under 21 minutes

PRACTICE
Brainstorming Buddies
Pairs interview each other to list information for their résumés.

- Partners ask these questions:
- *What paying jobs have you had? What non-paying ones?*
- *What are your hobbies? What skills did you learn from them?*
- *What computer programs do you know how to use?*
- *What are your best subjects in school?*
- *What accomplishments or awards set you apart?*
- Pairs list their answers.

☐ CLASS WORK ☐ HOMEWORK
☐ EXTRA CREDIT ☐ PROJECT

APPLY
Write a Résumé
- Students read the résumé, underlining relevant facts.
- Students write résumés.
- Partners exchange résumés, proofread, and correct errors.

Possible Answers INVESTIGATE:
3.0 grade-point average; starting pitcher, varsity baseball team; pitcher, junior varsity baseball team; pitcher, Dempsey Street Junior League; outfielder, Dempsey Street Minor League; after-school junior coach, Dempsey Street Boys' and Girls' Club. Answers for **WRITE** and **EVALUATE** will vary.

☐ CLASS WORK ☐ HOMEWORK
☐ EXTRA CREDIT ☐ PROJECT

EXTEND
Connect to Business Literacy
What job or career do you think you might like to have someday? Do you know what qualifications you will probably need to get the job—or what an average day on the job might be like? A good way to find out is to interview someone who has a job or career that interests you.

Make a list of at least five questions you would like to ask the person. Be sure to include a question about the qualifications needed for the job.

☐ CLASS WORK ☐ HOMEWORK
☐ EXTRA CREDIT ☐ PROJECT

Unit 1 Life Skills   23

NAME _____ DATE _____

Write a Résumé

INVESTIGATE ▶ A student saw an ad for coach assistant jobs. The jobs are at a baseball camp for children ages six through ten. The camp hires high-school students to assist its coaches. As you read the student's résumé, underline facts you think could help the student get the job.

84 WHY TRY? Because— I can write a winning résumé!

Gordon Glenn
800 West Jackson Street • Chicago, IL 61001
312-555-5501
E-mail: gglenn@example.com

Objective
To get a job related to baseball that will build on my experience and help me qualify to be a physical education teacher some day

Education
Currently in my sophomore year; 3.0 grade-point average
Roy West High School • 1090 Dempsey Road • Chicago 61001

Sports Experience
Present
Starting pitcher, Roy West High School varsity baseball team

2009
Pitcher, Roy West High School junior varsity baseball team

2007–2008
Pitcher, Dempsey Street Junior League

2002–2006
Outfielder, Dempsey Street Minor League

Coaching Experience
2008–Present
After-school junior coach: baseball, basketball
Dempsey Boys' and Girls' Club • 1301 Dempsey Street • Chicago 61001

References
• Coach Jack Jackson, Roy West High School, coach_jack@example.edu
• Ms. Kay Jones, Dempsey Boys' and Girls' Club, KGJ@example.org

---

WRITE ▶ What kind of summer job would you enjoy? In your Journal, write a résumé you could use to apply for the job. Use the résumé above as a model.

EVALUATE ▶ Exchange résumés with a partner. Proofread each other's work. Fix mistakes. Then word process your résumé, and proofread it again.

24 Lesson 84 Writing Résumés © 2011 Saddleback Educational Publishing

Writing Cover Letters and Thank-You Notes

85

INTRODUCE THINK ABOUT IT *How can you use formal business communication to both get a job interview and follow up after the interview?*

TEACH LISTEN UP! Consider **communication** "before" and "after" a job interview. Before you interview, you send a résumé and cover letter. The cover letter tells the employer how your strengths, skills, and experience make you right for the job, and details about the **qualities** that make you a good match for the position.

After the interview, you send a thank-you note to the person who interviewed you to thank him or her for the opportunity to interview, ask if he or she has any further questions, and offer to send any additional information the interviewer may need to consider.

LET'S EXPLORE Ask for volunteers to offer information about the format and content that should be presented in cover letters and thank-you notes. Write their ideas on the board. For example, both types of letters should:

- follow proper business letter format.
- be written clearly, with short paragraphs that get right to the point.
- be neatly typed, with correct spelling and grammar.

REVERSE Q & A Invite students to ask questions about the purposes of cover letters and thank-you notes, as well as details that should be included in them.

REFLECT *Do you think cover letters and thank-you notes can make a difference between who gets a job and who doesn't?*

▸ **Why write a cover letter if your résumé has your information?**
The cover letter is like an introduction to your résumé. It can also highlight both your personality and your communication skills.

▸ **What if you don't send a thank-you note?**
Example: An interviewer may think you are not serious about wanting the job.

WRITING COVER LETTERS AND THANK-YOU NOTES

LESSON OBJECTIVE
Write a cover letter and a post-interview thank-you note.

TERMS TO KNOW
communication: the sharing of information, often in the form of letters for business
qualities: character traits
GOES WELL WITH LESSONS: 29, 63, 91

21st Century Activities ... Each done in under 21 minutes

PRACTICE
Before and After
Partners brainstorm the details to include in cover letters and thank-you notes.

- Students form pairs. One partner is "before" and one is "after."
- Distribute **job ads** from the newspaper.
- Have partners spend 5 minutes brainstorming ideas. "Before" works on the cover letter, "after" works on the thank-you note for the job in the ad they were given.
- Tell students to spend the last few minutes of the activity sharing their ideas with each other.

☐ CLASS WORK ☐ HOMEWORK
☐ EXTRA CREDIT ☐ PROJECT

APPLY
Letter Writing
Individuals complete **Activity Sheet 85**.
- Read the cover letter aloud to students. Discuss any vocabulary with which they are unfamiliar.
- Students underline the key parts of the letter and fix spelling errors.
- Students then write their own thank-you notes in their **Journal (p. W3)**.

Possible Answers UNDERSTAND:
Underline sentences 2, 3, 7. Spelling errors: expirience, compny, sincerly. **WRITE:** Letter content will vary.

☐ CLASS WORK ☐ HOMEWORK
☐ EXTRA CREDIT ☐ PROJECT

EXTEND
Connect to Business Literacy
With so many people competing for jobs, it takes extra effort to stand out. A cover letter and thank-you note can help you stand above the rest.

Interview an adult in your life. Ask that person about his or her job. Take notes as the person tells about the background, experience, and skills someone with that job needs to have. Use your notes to write a cover letter, pretending that you have the same background, experience, and skills and are applying for that position.

☐ CLASS WORK ☐ HOMEWORK
☐ EXTRA CREDIT ☐ PROJECT

Unit 1 Life Skills   25

Letter Writing

INVESTIGATE Listen as your teacher reads the sample cover letter. Ask questions about any words you do not understand. Then, check to see that the writer has included:

- Strength, skills, and experience
- Why he is right for the job
- A formal business tone
- Proper business-letter format

Ms. Monique Newell
EDD Publishing Company
1212 Smith Drive
Marion, TX 47593

Dear Ms. Newell:

I'm writing in response to your ad for a position in your customer service department.

I have 15 years of customer service expirience. My last ten years were in the book publishing industry. My company was bought out by another compny. It then moved to a new location.

I have found working in book sales to be very rewarding. My leadership qualities and organizational skills have helped me in past positions. I would appreciate the opportunity to discuss with you how my skills and experience might benefit your company.

Sincerely,

Marcus Gray

Marcus Gray

UNDERSTAND Reread the cover letter. Underline the sentences or phrases that show the writer's strengths, skills, and experience.

Then, reread the letter to check for any errors in spelling or grammar. Fix any errors you find.

WRITE Now imagine that you have had the opportunity to interview for the job described above or your dream job. In your Journal, write a thank-you note you would send after the interview.

85 WHY TRY? Because— You want that job!

26 Lesson 85 Writing Cover Letters and Thank-You Notes © 2011 Saddleback Educational Publishing

Making a Good Impression

86

MAKING A GOOD IMPRESSION

INTRODUCE THINK ABOUT IT *Have you ever heard someone say, "Put your best foot forward"? What do you think it means?*

TEACH LISTEN UP! In a job interview, you answer questions. Your answers give the interviewer an idea of who you are, and what you know. But there are many other ways you are giving the interviewer information about who you are! Consider these:
- What you wear
- How you sit or stand
- How you speak

In this lesson, we'll discuss more about how to present yourself well to make a good impression.

LET'S EXPLORE Discuss tips for interviewing. Give guidelines on appearance and speech.
- Dress neatly in clothes that are clean, nothing too flashy or dressy; be well-groomed, have clean hair, fingernails, and teeth; make sure clothes are color coordinated and keep jewelry and make-up simple.
- Be aware of your **body language**; stand or sit up straight; make eye contact; practice a firm handshake while making eye contact.
- Speak clearly; think before speaking; when necessary, ask to clarify before responding; be able to back up your experience with references; thank the interviewer.

TIME FOR Q & A Discover more about how planning ahead can help you make a good impression.

▶ *How can preparing questions for the interviewer help you?*
It shows your interest in the job.

▶ *Why pick out clothes the night before?*
to make sure they are clean and presentable

▶ *Why should you set your travel route the night before?*
to make sure you arrive on time

▶ *Why bring an extra copy of your résumé and references?*
to show you're prepared and to supply extras to other interviewers

REFLECT *Is your appearance as important as what you say? Why or why not?*

LESSON OBJECTIVE
Apply interview do's and don'ts in mock interviews.

TERMS TO KNOW
body language: nonverbal communication, such as posture and gestures
clarify: to make clearer
impression: the way someone thinks of you
nonverbal: not spoken

GOES WELL WITH LESSONS:
26, 64, 84

21st Century Activities ... Each done in under 21 minutes

PRACTICE
Step Up
Have students practice making a good impression.
- Ask volunteers to role-play entering an office for a job interview.
- Playing the role of interviewer, check to see that students are making eye contact, delivering a firm handshake, and introducing themselves with a clear voice.
- You may also practice sitting and standing postures with students.
- Have students note what is working for each volunteer.

☐ CLASS WORK ☐ HOMEWORK
☐ EXTRA CREDIT ☐ PROJECT

APPLY
A Job Interview
Partners complete **Activity Sheet 86**.
- Have students read the interview scenario.
- Students identify the problems in *Understand*.
- Have partners work together to make recommendations for improvement in *Apply*.

Possible Answers APPLY: Brandon should have arrived on time after resting the night before; showed eye contact; offered references

☐ CLASS WORK ☐ HOMEWORK
☐ EXTRA CREDIT ☐ PROJECT

EXTEND
Connect to Global Awareness
A greeting can mean different things in different places. A handshake in the United States is the perfect way to say, "Nice to meet you." In another country, a handshake—or touching—may be considered rude.

Do an Internet search to find examples of greetings from different countries around the globe. Create a presentation of what you find, including images if they are available.

☐ CLASS WORK ☐ HOMEWORK
☐ EXTRA CREDIT ☐ PROJECT

Unit 2 Career Skills   27

NAME _____ DATE _____

A Job Interview

86 WHY TRY? Because— First impressions are important!

INVESTIGATE Read the summary of Brandon Pepper's job interview. As you read, think about the negative and positive points of his behavior during the interview.

On April 20, Brandon Pepper had a job interview at 10:00 a.m. He planned his travel route the night before. Brandon arrived at the office at 10:10 a.m. He introduced himself at the main desk and was led into the interviewer's office.

Brandon was so tired from being up late and then getting caught in traffic, he slumped down in his chair. He didn't shake the interviewer's hand, but he said hello.

Brandon wore a nice pair of pants and a collared shirt. He didn't think he needed to wear a tie. Brandon thought the questions went pretty well. But he was nervous, and he spoke more quickly than he realized. Brandon wasn't sure of all the questions, so he just made some of his answers up.

At the end of the interview, Brandon thanked the interviewer for his time.

UNDERSTAND Underline all the mistakes you think Brandon made. Then circle what he did well.

APPLY Discuss the guidelines for making a good impression as they apply to this interview. What would you tell Brandon to do differently? Write your ideas on the lines below.

_____
_____
_____
_____
_____
_____
_____
_____
_____

28   Lesson 86 Making a Good Impression   © 2011 Saddleback Educational Publishing

Applying Learning Styles

87

INTRODUCE THINK ABOUT IT *Did you know that people learn best in different ways? Which way do you learn best?*

TEACH LISTEN UP! There are three main learning styles:

- **Visual learners** learn by watching and seeing. They should try to make mind-pictures of the information they learn. Graphs help them learn. They study best in visually bland surroundings.
- **Auditory learners** learn by hearing. They should try to repeat aloud what they learn and read information aloud. They should put information in their own words. They study best in quiet surroundings.
- **Kinesthetic learners** need to be active. They should try to connect information with an action. They remember information that requires action (such as how-tos) best. They study best when they take frequent, active breaks.

Ask: *Which learning style do you think best describes the way you learn? Let's each do the Identify portion of Activity Sheet 87 to find out.*

LET'S EXPLORE As a class, brainstorm a list of recently learned skills and information. (Examples of activities: how to skateboard, how to download MP3 files, how to play a game. Examples of topics: U.S. political process, history of the Civil Rights movement, geology of Yellowstone Park, or any other topic explored in class.) Discuss how different students learned similar information and whether or not that learning method matches the results of their learning style surveys in **Activity Sheet 87**.

THINK, PAIR, SHARE Have pairs of students who have learned the same skill or studied the same topic discuss the approach they used. How well did each approach work? Did they wish they would have used a different approach? Call on random pairs to share their thoughts.

REFLECT *Which tasks match your learning style the best? Which might be difficult?*

APPLYING LEARNING STYLES

LESSON OBJECTIVE
Identify individual learning style and brainstorm ways to apply it.

TERMS TO KNOW
auditory: related to the sense of hearing
kinesthetic: related to movement
visual: related to the sense of sight

GOES WELL WITH LESSONS:
13, 40, 99

21st Century Activities ... Each done in under 21 minutes

PRACTICE
Learning Out Loud
Students discuss each situation below and how they can adapt it for an auditory learning style.
- Learn a computer program. (Have somebody explain.)
- Memorize a list of facts. (Say it aloud repeatedly.)
- Learn to drive. (Have somebody explain each step.)
- Learn an instrument. (Listen to a taped explanation.)
- Learn to ride a bicycle on curves and hills. (Find a video online and pay particular attention to the audio explanation.)

☐ CLASS WORK ☐ HOMEWORK
☐ EXTRA CREDIT ☐ PROJECT

APPLY
What's My Learning Style?
Individuals complete **Activity Sheet 87**.
- After identifying your learning style, create a learning plan.

Possible Answers For *DESIGN* answers will vary.
- Visual: Make mind pictures. Study in a visually bland place.
- Auditory: Say things aloud in my own words. Study in a quiet area.
- Kinesthetic: Connect ideas to movement. Take frequent breaks.

Teacher Tip: To extend the activity, students can research online for specific study strategies that are right for their learning styles.

☐ CLASS WORK ☐ HOMEWORK
☐ EXTRA CREDIT ☐ PROJECT

EXTEND
Connect to Health Literacy
Over time, U.S. lifestyles have become less and less active, and schools are no different. People who are kinesthetic learners often struggle in learning environments in which they have to sit the entire time.

Develop a way to learn current content from another class for a kinesthetic learner. The study method should include physical activity, such as dance or a connection between certain movements and facts to be learned.

Groups present their learning method to the class.

☐ CLASS WORK ☐ HOMEWORK
☐ EXTRA CREDIT ☐ PROJECT

Unit 2 Career Skills

What's My Learning Style?

WHY TRY? Because— People learn in different ways!

INVESTIGATE ▶ Everyone has a learning style, and there are study methods that can help you make the most of yours. These strategies not only help you learn better, they help you learn faster. If you use strategies that match your learning style, you might find it easier to learn material in school.

IDENTIFY ▶ To discover your learning style, circle the letter that follows each statement that is true for you.

- When I read, I often whisper the words out loud. (A)
- I have a very active imagination and "see" things in my mind. (V)
- If I had to pick one hobby, it would be painting and drawing. (V)
- If I had to pick one hobby, it would be sports or dancing. (K)
- If I had to pick one hobby, it would be playing an instrument or singing. (A)
- In conversation, I touch people a lot. (K)
- I often talk to myself out loud. (A)
- I hum or whistle while I work. (A)
- I doodle a lot. (V)
- I always remember faces. (V)
- I almost never sit still. (K)
- People tell me I talk with my hands. (K)

Results

Mostly As: You are likely an auditory learner. You learn best by hearing information.

Mostly Vs: You are likely a visual learner. You learn best by seeing information and making pictures in your mind.

Mostly Ks: You are likely a kinesthetic learner. You learn best when movement is involved.

DESIGN ▶ Develop a learning plan that is right for you. Think of a learning task that you sometimes struggle with, such as studying for tests or remembering how to spell certain words. In your Journal, write some ways that you can improve your approach to that learning task based on your learning style.

Being Independent

88

INTRODUCE THINK ABOUT IT *In what way is working independently an important skill?*

TEACH LISTEN UP! Managers are busy people. They have many concerns beyond just supervising employees. Employees who are **independent** soon become highly valued workers. There are many ways to be and to show that you are an independent worker:

- Take notes at meetings or when you are given directions. If you are confused, ask questions. This will ensure you have the information you need to start your task.
- Learn about the company you work for and how you can help the company reach its goals. This will keep you focused.
- Take **initiative**. Lead yourself in taking action that is **productive** for the company. Offer suggestions for improving ways that things are done.
- Have a plan for **downtime**. Keep a list of things you can do next time there is a break in your duties.

LET'S EXPLORE As a class, discuss the scene below.

Susan's boss just explained a new 6-step procedure to her and her coworkers. Susan was the only person who took written notes. What could she do that would show initiative? (Possible Answer: She could type up the notes and submit them to her boss and coworkers.)

PLAY THESE ROLES A manager and an employee talk about time the employee has been spending surfing the Internet when she is not busy at work.

▸ *How can the employee make better use of downtime?*
She can ask the manager for extra tasks that can help her get ahead in the company.

▸ *How can the manager inspire the employee to work harder?*
She can let the employee know that her work is very important to the company's success.

REFLECT *How can you make constructive use of downtime at work or during study breaks?*

BEING INDEPENDENT

LESSON OBJECTIVE
Apply workplace skills that promote independence.

TERMS TO KNOW
downtime: a time period at work when an employee has no important tasks to do
independent: able to work by oneself without being supervised; not relying on others for support
initiative: the ability to suggest or do actions that create positive results
productive: having the ability to create positive results

GOES WELL WITH LESSONS:
23, 43, 74

21st Century Activities ... Each done in under 21 minutes

PRACTICE
Productive Criticism
- The class observes a small group that is playing the roles of a project team and a teacher.
- The teacher is frustrated about missed deadlines. In class, there has been more talk than work.
- The teacher asks what she can do to help the team make deadlines. Team members respond.
- The rest of the class discusses whether the meeting was productive.

Teacher suggestion: Discuss the importance of taking criticism and doing better in the future.

☐ CLASS WORK ☐ HOMEWORK
☐ EXTRA CREDIT ☐ PROJECT

APPLY
Being Independent
Individuals complete **Activity Sheet 88**.
- Read. Then, make notes based on the passage and a to-do list based on the notes.
- Evaluate the conversation between Tomás and his boss.
- Distribute the **Journal (p. W3)**.

Possible Answers Notes in *ANALYZE* will vary. To-do list: **1.** Move TVs from Building A to Building C. **2.** Record change on Building A inventory. **3.** Record change on Building C inventory.

☐ CLASS WORK ☐ HOMEWORK
☐ EXTRA CREDIT ☐ PROJECT

EXTEND
Connect to Business Literacy
People who are able to work independently and who have initiative could go far in the business world.

You overheard that the owner of the sandwich café where you work is looking for new menu ideas that will appeal to a younger crowd. Come up with an idea and then create an ad that shows why young people will enjoy the sandwich. Include images (hand-drawn, cut from **magazines**, or electronic) and text in your ad. Make your ad on **paper** or on the **computer**.

☐ CLASS WORK ☐ HOMEWORK
☐ EXTRA CREDIT ☐ PROJECT

Unit 2 Career Skills

Being Independent

INVESTIGATE One way to become an independent employee is to listen carefully and take notes. Read the following conversation between Tomás and his supervisor.

Tomás is a new employee in a warehouse. So far, he's spent most of his time stacking crates with a forklift. This morning, the foreman said, "You need to make room for a new shipment, Tomás. Move the TVs that are in Building A to Building C. Stack them up on the top level."

"We've got TVs in Buildings A, B, *and* C," Tomás told him. "You want me to move *all* of them to C?"

"No," the foreman said. "Just the ones here in A."

"Then I'll need to enter it on the inventory for Building C, right?"

"Right," said the foreman. "You also need to show them leaving Building A, so it goes on that inventory as well."

"You want me to move them right away?" Tomás asked.

"Yep, just as soon as you can," the foreman replied.

ANALYZE In the space below, write down the notes you think Tomás might have taken, based on the directions from his foreman. Then, create a to-do list for Tomás, based on the notes.

_____
_____
_____
_____
_____
_____
_____

JUDGE In your Journal, evaluate the conversation between Tomás and his boss. Do you think that Tomás asked enough questions while speaking with his boss? Do you think he asked too many questions? Do you think the notes you took and the to-do list you made would help Tomás complete the work independently? Is there anything else Tomás could have done to impress his boss even more?

88 WHY TRY? Because— I am independent!

Prioritizing Your Work

89

PRIORITIZING YOUR WORK

INTRODUCE THINK ABOUT IT *Did you know that every busy person must prioritize tasks?*

TEACH LISTEN UP! Over the course of a day or a week, many tasks and responsibilities compete for time. A to-do list that organizes each task by its **priority** is a great tool to help you get things done. When you determine a task's prioriity, ask yourself the following questions:
- Is this task **urgent**?
- Is this task important?

Tasks that are both **urgent** and important are usually high-priority activities. Tasks that are one or the other usually have a medium priority, and tasks that are neither urgent or important are usually low-level priorities.

LET'S EXPLORE As a class, explore the concept of priorities.
- Make a 3-column chart on the board. Label the columns *High, Medium,* and *Low.*
- As a group, brainstorm lists of students' high-, medium-, and low-priority tasks.
- As a task is mentioned for each list, discuss why it falls into that category and whether another student might put it in a different column.

TIME FOR Q & A Discover more about competing priorities.

▸ *What priority level should health concerns like eating well and exercising have? Do you think most people pay attention to these concerns? Why or why not?*

▸ *When you do not have enough time to get everything done, how do you make good choices about what you leave out? How could you do better?*

REFLECT *How can you prioritize tasks so that high priorities are met even when they are not urgent?*

LESSON OBJECTIVE
Prioritize tasks according to level of urgency and importance.

TERMS TO KNOW
priority: something that gets attention before other concerns
urgent: calls for immediate attention

GOES WELL WITH LESSONS:
23, 54, 90

21st Century Activities ... Each done in under 21 minutes

PRACTICE
Money Matters
Paying bills is an important task that becomes urgent if it is ignored. Make a plan to prioritize finances.
- Give students a **monthly bills and income statement:** Rent: $550, Utilities: $80, Cell phone: $100, Food: $250, Car payment: $175, Insurance: $95. Pay: $450 every Friday.
- Give students a **calendar** with notes on each Friday: Pay: _____, Save: _____, and Spend: _____.
- Provide help as needed.

☐ CLASS WORK ☐ HOMEWORK
☐ EXTRA CREDIT ☐ PROJECT

APPLY
Make a Prioritized To-Do List
Individuals complete **Activity Sheet 89.**
- Individuals make a prioritized to-do list.
- Students reflect on the prioritized to-do list as a tool and how it can be effective in their lives.

Possible Answers Answers for *LIST* and *COMPARE* will vary. With a prioritized to-do list, students will probably get more done. When they do not get everything done, they will have a good way to make decisions about what can wait for another day.

☐ CLASS WORK ☐ HOMEWORK
☐ EXTRA CREDIT ☐ PROJECT

EXTEND
Connect to Environmental Literacy
Large organizations, like corporations and governments, are no different from individuals when it comes to setting priorities. Often important issues—such as environmental responsibility—are not as urgent as making money or running a country.

Write a letter to a local business or government agency explaining why they should make a specific environmental concern a higher priority over some other issues. If possible, mail your letter.

☐ CLASS WORK ☐ HOMEWORK
☐ EXTRA CREDIT ☐ PROJECT

Unit 2 Prioritizing Your Work

NAME _____ DATE _____

Make a Prioritized To-Do List

89 WHY TRY? Because— Set priorities to get things done!

INVESTIGATE Make a prioritized to-do list.

Sometimes life gets busy and many tasks compete for our time. To be successful, it is necessary to set priorities. By deciding if a task is a high, medium or low priority, you can better plan for the day, week, month, or even your whole life! A prioritized to-do list is a great tool for helping you move toward your goals.

LIST In the to-do list below, write several tasks that compete for your time. In the column next to the tasks, indicate whether each item is a high-priority, medium-priority, or low-priority task.

Task	Is it important?	Is it urgent?	Priority Level

COMPARE By answering the following questions, compare the prioritized to-do list method with the way you have been setting priorities up to now:

1. Have you written a to-do list before? If so, was it prioritized? Why or why not?
   _____
   _____

2. Will you keep a prioritized to-do list as you move forward in your life? Why or why not?
   _____
   _____

3. How do you think your life will be different in 5 years if you keep a daily prioritized to-do list?
   _____
   _____

Managing Your Time

INTRODUCE **THINK ABOUT IT** *Have you ever felt as if there aren't enough hours in the day to reach your goals? What are some ways to manage, or use, your time better?*

TEACH **LISTEN UP!** Managing time is a challenge for everyone. But with a plan in place, you can get more done in less time. A **prioritized** weekly **schedule** that includes **benchmarks** can make all the difference. To make a schedule, follow these steps:

1. **Establish Your Goals** List what you want to accomplish, or your goals, for the week.
2. **Set Priorities** Evaluate your list. Ask yourself: *Which of these are truly important?* Highlight or underline them. Then ask: *Could I drop any items?* Remove those items.
3. **Set Benchmarks** In order to reach a goal, set benchmarks, or ways you can check your progress, for specific days. For example, if you want to read a 120-page book in a week, you could set benchmarks of reading 40 pages on Monday, Wednesday, and Friday. You will have to meet each benchmark to reach your goal.

LET'S EXPLORE As a class, develop a list of typical student responsibilities and activities.
- Together, brainstorm goals for a workweek, on a **Checklist (p. W6)** or on the board.
- Students should copy the goals and then highlight or underline items that are priorities.
- Point out that priorities may differ from student to student. Have students compare theirs.
- Have students write one or two benchmarks they could set to help reach a priority goal.

TIME FOR Q & A To further the discussion of time management, ask these questions.

▶ *Why do people sometimes fail to achieve their goals? Is it their fault or the fault of a schedule?* It could be both. People may not feel like doing their work, or they may have allowed too little time to do something.

▶ *How can you improve a schedule?* Adding benchmarks to your schedule can help you check on the progress you are making to reach a goal.

REFLECT *How can setting benchmarks help you manage your time?*

90
MANAGING YOUR TIME

LESSON OBJECTIVE
Make a prioritized list of goals and benchmarks.

TERMS TO KNOW
benchmark: a way to check that you are reaching your goal
priority: a task having a higher level of importance than other tasks
schedule: a listing of the times at which things are done or will be done

GOES WELL WITH LESSONS:
16, 64, 89

21st Century Activities ... Each done in under 21 minutes

PRACTICE
Practice Scheduling a Project With the class, create a schedule for a school project.
- Give students a hypothetical goal to achieve, such as completing a research report.
- Set a deadline for the finished product.
- Together, brainstorm benchmarks that students could set to achieve the goal.
- List the benchmarks on the board.
- Students use the benchmarks to make a weekly schedule. Use the **Planner (p. W11)**.

☐ CLASS WORK ☐ HOMEWORK
☐ EXTRA CREDIT ☐ PROJECT

APPLY
Reaching Goals in Record Time
Individuals complete **Activity Sheet 90**.
- In their **Journal (p. W3)**, students list goals they would like to achieve.
- Students pick their priorities and decide on benchmarks.
- After making a schedule, students answer questions to evaluate and possibly revise their schedules.

Possible Answers Schedules will vary but should be complete and show an understanding of how to set priorities and benchmarks.

☐ CLASS WORK ☐ HOMEWORK
☐ EXTRA CREDIT ☐ PROJECT

EXTEND
Connect to Health Literacy
Do you schedule time to do healthful activities, such as exercising? Schedule a good new habit today!

Think of free or unscheduled times in your week. List the times, for example, *I am free for an hour between 4:30 p.m. and 5:30 p.m. on Tuesday*. Then brainstorm ways you can exercise during that time. Set a goal for the week, such as walking six miles. You can set benchmarks during the week to break up the total amount of miles.

☐ CLASS WORK ☐ HOMEWORK
☐ EXTRA CREDIT ☐ PROJECT

Unit 2 Career Skills 35

NAME _____ DATE _____

Reaching Goals in Record Time

90 WHY TRY? Because— I can manage my time!

INVESTIGATE ▶ In your Journal, list the goals you want to accomplish next week. Highlight or underline goals that are priorities. Then set benchmarks, or ways to check your progress, for each priority goal.

SCHEDULE ▶ Use two or three of your top priority goals to fill out the schedule below. Add hours if you need to. Start by deciding a final day and date for each goal. Then, add the benchmarks on days leading up to the final day. Make sure you can accomplish all of the steps to reach each goal.

	Sunday	Monday	Tuesday	Wednesday	Thursday	Friday	Saturday
all-day							
9 AM							
10 AM							
11 AM							
NOON							
1 PM							
2 PM							
3 PM							
4 PM							
5 PM							
6 PM							
7 PM							
8 PM							

EVALUATE ▶ In your Journal, evaluate your schedule by answering the questions.

1. Will I stick to my schedule? Are my benchmarks realistic? Why or why not?
2. How would you reschedule your week if a new priority came up?
3. How can you evaluate if the week's benchmarks were appropriate for each goal?

Lesson 90 Managing Your Time © 2011 Saddleback Educational Publishing

Writing a Business Letter

91
WRITING A BUSINESS LETTER

INTRODUCE **THINK ABOUT IT** *Have you ever needed to write a letter to request information, file a complaint, or apply for a job? How did you go about doing it?*

TEACH **LISTEN UP!** Remind students that a business letter is a type of formal, written communication that is used to do a business transaction, such as asking for information, filing a complaint, or requesting a job interview. The main parts of a business letter are as follows:

- **Heading:** the sender's address
- **Inside address:** the address to which the letter is to be sent
- **Greeting:** an appropriate opening, such as *Dear Sir*
- **Body:** the message
- **Closing:** an appropriate conclusion, such as *Sincerely* or *Yours truly*
- **Signature:** the sender's signed name

LET'S EXPLORE Point out that a complaint letter is a common kind of business letter. Like all business letters, it should be written in a formal, respectful **tone**. A complaint letter is not just an angry opinion. It should include facts, reasons, and examples to help the business understand the problem that caused the complaint.

- Ask students to describe situations that would require a letter of complaint.
- Write *facts, reasons,* and *examples* on the board and have students give an example of each.

THINK, PAIR, SHARE Explain that writing a complaint letter is an opportunity to speak up and be heard. Have students discuss a real or invented complaint with a partner. Tell them to think of facts, reasons, and examples that support their complaint. Ask partners to report their ideas to the whole group after discussion.

REFLECT *How can a well-written business letter help you resolve a complaint?*

LESSON OBJECTIVE
Apply business-writing basics to write a complaint letter.

TERMS TO KNOW
tone: a writer's attitude toward his or her audience and subject as shown in his or her choice of words

GOES WELL WITH LESSONS:
29, 63, 98

21st Century Activities ... Each done in under 21 minutes

PRACTICE
Watch Your Tone
Partners revise sentences with accusatory or threatening tones.

- On the board, write statements that display an inappropriate tone for a business complaint letter. For example, *Are you guys stupid, or is it that you just don't care about customers?*
- Ask volunteers to describe how they would feel if they received a letter with the statements. Would they be motivated to help the customer?
- Pairs revise the sentences.

☐ CLASS WORK ☐ HOMEWORK
☐ EXTRA CREDIT ☐ PROJECT

APPLY
Revise a Business Letter
Individuals complete **Activity Sheet 91**.
- Students read and analyze the tone of the letter.
- Students use the **Journal (p. W3)** to revise the letter to correct the tone.

Possible Answers ANALYZE: "What's up with that?"; "In fact, your salespeople seem to know nothing about the clothes you sell!"; "The next time I am shopping for new clothes, I will be going somewhere else!"
REVISE: Students' revisions will vary but should be written in an appropriate tone for a business letter.

☐ CLASS WORK ☐ HOMEWORK
☐ EXTRA CREDIT ☐ PROJECT

EXTEND
Connect to Business Literacy
Imagine that you are the owner of a business. What rules do you want your employees to follow when they handle complaints?

Brainstorm a list of at least five rules. For each rule, give a rationale, or reason, for example, *You should be polite because we don't want to hurt our customers' feelings or make them angry.* Present your list of rules and reasons to the class. Be prepared to answer questions.

☐ CLASS WORK ☐ HOMEWORK
☐ EXTRA CREDIT ☐ PROJECT

Unit 2 Career Skills

Revise a Business Letter

91 WHY TRY? Because— I have the right to be heard!

INVESTIGATE Read the complaint letter below.

Mr. Alberto Martinez
1090 West Avenue
Palm Tree City, Florida 32000

January 10, 2012

Mr. Jermaine Hudson
Dollar Discount Palace
5030 Penny Street
Palm Tree City, Florida 32000

Dear Mr. Hudson:

Usually, I enjoy shopping at Dollar Discount Palace. But last week, I was very disappointed when I went there.

Your ads said that all clothes were on sale. But when I got to the store, only some things were marked down. What's up with that? I talked to a salesperson, but I didn't get any answers from her. In fact, your salespeople seem to know nothing about the clothes you sell! I was not at all satisfied with the customer service.

The next time I am shopping for new clothes, I will be going somewhere else!

Sincerely,

Mr. Alberto Martinez

Mr. Alberto Martinez

ANALYZE At some points in the letter, the writer used the wrong tone. Underline sentences that have a bad or unpleasant tone. Remember that the tone is the writer's attitude toward his or her audience and subject as shown in the choice of words.

REVISE In your Journal, rewrite the letter so that it has a friendly, appropriate tone.

Lesson 91 Writing a Business Letter
© 2011 Saddleback Educational Publishing

Writing a Proposal

92

WRITING A PROPOSAL

INTRODUCE THINK ABOUT IT *Have you ever needed to share a good idea with the students at your school? What would be the best way to do this?*

TEACH LISTEN UP! A proposal is a good way to share an idea in writing. Proposals are business documents, so the language is formal and the format is like a memo. A proposal has four parts, and each part answers one of the following questions:

- **Summary** What is suggested?
- **Benefits** Why do it?
- **Resources** What is needed?
- **Timeline** When will each part happen?

Consider your audience when writing a proposal. The aim is to present your idea convincingly, so your audience will approve the proposal.

LET'S EXPLORE Ask students what information they would include in a proposal for a school fund-raiser. Help students complete each section, such as the following:

- Summary: propose a school reading program
- Benefits: to encourage students to read more
- Resources: we need a location and volunteers to help out
- Timeline: our fundraiser would take one afternoon

TIME FOR Q & A Discover more about the purpose of a proposal.

▸ *Why consider the audience?*
because the reader can approve or deny your request

▸ *Why include strong reasons?*
Strong reasons persuade the reader.

▸ *Why put it in writing?*
The reader can consider the benefits before making a decision.

▸ *Why not just make a phone call?*
A proposal is a formal record.

REFLECT *What idea would you like to propose to students?*

LESSON OBJECTIVE
Write a proposal on a school-related topic.

TERMS TO KNOW
benefits: good or helpful results
proposal: a business document that sets forth a plan or suggestion
resources: things that can be used to accomplish something

GOES WELL WITH LESSONS:
29, 63, 93

21st Century Activities ... Each done in under 21 minutes

PRACTICE
Win It in a Minute
Pair students and tell them they will have a minute to "sell" an idea to a partner. Tell students to share:

- the proposed idea
- 2–3 benefits

Then have each partner approve or deny the proposal, and explain why. After one minute, have students switch partners and repeat the process. Encourage students to support each other's ideas and ask volunteers to share approved ideas with the group after the game has ended.

☐ CLASS WORK   ☐ HOMEWORK
☐ EXTRA CREDIT   ☐ PROJECT

APPLY
Proposal: Approve or Deny
Individuals complete **Activity Sheet 92**.

- Read aloud the sample proposal.
- Have students analyze the proposal, filling in the chart as they identify the parts.
- Tell students to approve or deny the proposal and have them explain their answer to a partner.

Possible Answers ANALYZE: Summary – a walk-a-thon fund-raiser. Benefits – low-cost, encourages physical activity, raises money for P.E. program, kids won't miss school. Resources – school track, volunteers. Timeline – one week to plan and one afternoon for the event. **EVALUATE:** Answers will vary.

☐ CLASS WORK   ☐ HOMEWORK
☐ EXTRA CREDIT   ☐ PROJECT

EXTEND
Connect to Health Literacy
Imagine that your school is considering holding a health fair. The fair will include booths and activities promoting healthful habits.

Work with a small group to draft a proposal for the health fair that will include booths and activities you think will be helpful and fun. Include your ideas for the fair, the benefits of your ideas, the resources needed, and the timeline for planning and carrying out the fair.

☐ CLASS WORK   ☐ HOMEWORK
☐ EXTRA CREDIT   ☐ PROJECT

Unit 2 Career Skills   39

NAME _____ DATE _____

Proposal: Approve or Deny

92 WHY TRY? Because— I've got a good idea to share!

INVESTIGATE Read the proposal. As you read, look for evidence that the writer included a summary, the benefits, the resources, and a timeline.

Date: April 4, 2012

To: Principal Calley

From: Turner School Council

It's time for our school council to begin planning this year's spring fund-raiser. We would like to propose a walk-a-thon. A walk-a-thon is a great idea for several reasons. First, it would keep costs low. We can hold our walk-a-thon on the school track, and we don't need any special equipment. Second, a walk-a-thon supports our school goal of increasing physical fitness. And a fitness activity is a great idea because we are raising money to support our school's P.E. program. Finally, we can hold this event on a Saturday afternoon so no one will miss school in order to attend!

Principal Calley, we think you'll agree that a walk-a-thon is the best idea for this year's fund-raiser. Please let us know if you will approve our proposal.

ANALYZE Complete the chart, giving examples from the proposal for each section. At the bottom of the chart, circle *Approve* or *Deny*, and explain your answer.

SUMMARY	
BENEFITS	
RESOURCES	
TIMELINE	
APPROVE or DENY	

EVALUATE Defend your opinion to a classmate. Tell a partner if you approved or denied the proposal, and explain your answer using evidence from your chart.

Lesson 92 Writing a Proposal © 2011 Saddleback Educational Publishing

Writing a Business E-mail

93

WRITING A BUSINESS E-MAIL

INTRODUCE **THINK ABOUT IT** *How does technology make business communication quicker and easier?*

TEACH **LISTEN UP!** Ask: *How many of you regularly use e-mail to communicate with friends or family?* E-mail is often used for business communication, too. These guidelines will help you write clear business e-mail:
1. **Keep it short.** Business e-mail gets right to the point.
2. **Check your facts.** Include all necessary information and make sure the information is accurate.
3. **Use a professional tone.** Business e-mail requires a formal, not casual, tone.
4. **Proofread.** Reread e-mail to check for mistakes before sending it.

When a quick reply is needed, business e-mail is an efficient way to communicate.

LET'S EXPLORE Brainstorm some situations that might require a business e-mail.
- Write students' ideas—such as sending a price quote, notifying a customer of a delay, asking for feedback, and so on—on the board.
- Discuss the four guidelines for writing business e-mails as they relate to student ideas.

REVERSE Q & A Students discover more about the purpose of business e-mails. Encourage students to ask questions about the purpose or the format of a business e-mail.

▸ *How do you decide whether to send an e-mail or a letter?*
Letters are for formal situations that do not require a quick reply.

▸ *What if I don't have the e-mail address?*
You may send a letter instead.

▸ *Should I send another e-mail if I don't get a response?* Any follow-up e-mail should also follow the business e-mail format.

▸ *Do I write an e-mail in the same format as a letter?* An e-mail does not require a date, heading, or inside address.

REFLECT *What are the differences between an e-mail to a friend and a business e-mail?*

LESSON OBJECTIVE
Apply basic e-mail rules to write a business e-mail.

TERMS TO KNOW
communication: an exchange of thoughts and ideas
efficient: the best way to get a job done
professional: related to business
proofread: to read carefully in order to find errors

GOES WELL WITH LESSONS:
28, 63, 91

21st Century Activities ... Each done in under 21 minutes

PRACTICE
Who's It To?
Help students identify the correct use of business e-mail.
- Give each student two **Index Cards (p. W10).** Have students write the names or titles of different people, such as Aunt Mary or Congressman Jones, on the cards.
- Choose index cards at random and read the name or title aloud.
- Ask students to show a "thumbs up" if the person requires a business e-mail. Have them show a "thumbs down" if a business e-mail is not needed.

☐ CLASS WORK ☐ HOMEWORK
☐ EXTRA CREDIT ☐ PROJECT

APPLY
Write an E-mail
Individuals complete **Activity Sheet 93.**
- Read aloud the business e-mail.
- Students identify the errors and explain how the e-mail could be improved.
- Students revise the e-mail so that it follows the guidelines for a business e-mail.

Possible Answers 1. Yes. **2.** No. What type of information about classes does he need? **3.** No. **4.** No. **CREATE:** Revised e-mails should use formal language, correct spelling and usage, and include the necessary information.

☐ CLASS WORK ☐ HOMEWORK
☐ EXTRA CREDIT ☐ PROJECT

EXTEND
Connect to Civic Literacy
Many people rely on the efficiency of business e-mail to communicate with local, state, and national politicians.

Choose an issue that is important to you, such as global warming or the need for a local recycling program. Draft a business e-mail to a local, state, or national leader, such as the President of the United States or our town mayor, explaining why this issue is important and asking him or her to take action to fix the problem.

☐ CLASS WORK ☐ HOMEWORK
☐ EXTRA CREDIT ☐ PROJECT

Unit 2 Career Skills

NAME _____ DATE _____

Write an E-mail

INVESTIGATE Read the business e-mail.

93 WHY TRY? Because— I've got a message to send!

To: student_advisor@college.edu

From: michael_denton@script.com

Subject: classes

Hey,

What's up? I'm planning my schedule for next year and I need to get the info on classes. You got that? If yes, can you shoot me a copy? If no, where do I get it?

Thx,

michael

IDENTIFY Identify the ways this business e-mail could be improved.

Did the writer...

1. keep it short? _____
2. include all the necessary information? _____
3. use a professional tone? _____
4. carefully proofread his e-mail? _____

CREATE Revise Michael's e-mail to write a business e-mail that follows the correct format. Proofread your work for correct spelling and punctuation.

_____
_____
_____
_____
_____
_____
_____

Lesson 93 Writing a Business E-mail   © 2011 Saddleback Educational Publishing

Thinking About the Customer

94

INTRODUCE THINK ABOUT IT *Do you realize that the customer is the business?*

TEACH LISTEN UP! With no customer, there is no company. Without a company, there are no jobs. Therefore, customer service is everybody's concern. To provide great customer service, follow these DOs and DON'Ts:

- DO put yourself in the customer's place.
- DO find a solution if there is a problem.
- DO show **appreciation**. With no customer, there is no job!
- DON'T speak against the company. Instead, show **loyalty**.
- DON'T get angry. Stay calm.
- DON'T take things personally—especially customer frustration!

LET'S EXPLORE As a class, discuss times when students had bad customer service.

- Invite students to offer brief stories of times when they received bad customer service, such as at a restaurant or store. If necessary, share a story of your own to get them started.
- Ask students to describe how they were feeling after the incident.
- Finally, ask students how they would have done things differently if they had been the clerk, restaurant server, or other customer service representative.

PLAY THESE ROLES Pose this situation: a customer can't hook up a DVD player and has called your customer service center. Have partners play roles. Follow up with these questions:

▸ *Put yourself in the customer's position. How was he or she feeling?*
Example: frustrated, angry, perhaps a bit embarrassed

▸ *Which DOs did the employee follow?*
Example: The employee found the solution of sending a new cord.

REFLECT *Can you think of a time when great customer service won your loyalty?*

THINKING ABOUT THE CUSTOMER

LESSON OBJECTIVE
Apply a list of DOs and DON'Ts to working with customers.

TERMS TO KNOW
appreciation: an expression of admiration, approval, or gratitude
loyalty: unchanging faith in a cause

GOES WELL WITH LESSONS:
20, 55, 91

21st Century Activities ... Each done in under 21 minutes

PRACTICE
Service? What Service?
Small groups work together to re-train a bad customer service representative.
- One student plays the role of a cashier in a grocery store. She is distracted by her cell phone and rushes through the order, barely speaking to the customer.
- Another student is the elderly customer who does not hear well and cannot find his check-card.
- The rest of the class points out which DO's and DON'Ts the cashier didn't follow and provide suggestions for ways she could have done things differently.

☐ CLASS WORK ☐ HOMEWORK
☐ EXTRA CREDIT ☐ PROJECT

APPLY
Instant Replay
Individuals complete **Activity Sheet 94**.
- Read aloud the customer service scene. Then have students reflect on what the clerk did wrong in *Analyze*.
- Students respond to the *Evaluate* questions in their **Journal (p. W3)**.

Possible Answers 1. She didn't think about how frustrated Jon might be. **2.** She did not find a solution. **3.** She did not thank Rohan for bringing up the locker room door problem. **4.** She made a negative comment about her boss. **5.** She got angry and upset. **6.** She took Rohan's frustration personally. **7-8.** Answers will vary.

☐ CLASS WORK ☐ HOMEWORK
☐ EXTRA CREDIT ☐ PROJECT

EXTEND
Connect to Business Literacy
To help resolve customer-relations issues when you are the customer, be polite but take a stand.

Think of a time when you were disappointed in a product or service. Write a letter to the company's customer service department explaining the problem and asking that it be solved. Use a polite tone, but make sure you take a stand for your own view of the situation. Use the proper business letter format. If appropriate, send the letter and see if you get a response.

☐ CLASS WORK ☐ HOMEWORK
☐ EXTRA CREDIT ☐ PROJECT

Unit 2 Career Skills

NAME _____ DATE _____

Instant Replay

INVESTIGATE Remember, with no customer, there is no company. With no company, there are no jobs. Always practice the DOs and DON'Ts of great customer service. Read this customer service scene and think about what the clerk could have done differently.

94 WHY TRY? Because— With no customer, there's no job!

Rohan approached the front desk at his gym. He knew right away that the clerk was in a dark mood. She was slumped back in her chair with a furrowed brow, and she was texting frantically. Rohan waited a second, but he was in a hurry. "Excuse me, Miss?"

The clerk looked up. Rohan was shocked to see her eyes roll slightly. "I can't seem to get my key card to work," Jon said. "Can you help me get into the locker room?"

"That again?" the clerk said. "I've been telling the manager that we need to have that machine fixed. I don't think he ever really hears a word I say." About then, the clerk's cell phone went off. Rohan knew she had just received another text and that she was now thinking of that.

"You must be really frustrated," Rohan said sarcastically.

"I really am!" the clerk replied, missing the point.

"Me, too," Rohan said, losing his temper. "And I can tell that you're busy with your texting and all, but I need to get into the locker room. I have to take a shower and get to work. Can you help me, or do I need to speak with your supervisor?"

"Well, excuse me!" the clerk said, her eyes flashing angrily. "This is not my fault. And I'm sorry, but I don't have a key to the men's locker room. Maybe if you wait at the door somebody will come by and his key card will work. I just don't think I can help you."

ANALYZE How did the clerk fail to follow each of the six DOs and DON'Ts of customer service?

1. _____
2. _____
3. _____
4. _____
5. _____
6. _____

EVALUATE Pretend you are the clerk's supervisor and that you just overheard her conversation with Rohan. Answer these questions in your Journal.

7. What would you say to the customer?
8. What would you say to the clerk after the customer had left?

44 Lesson 94 Thinking About the Customer   © 2011 Saddleback Educational Publishing

Resolving Conflicts at Work

95

RESOLVING CONFLICTS AT WORK

INTRODUCE THINK ABOUT IT *How can resolving conflicts at work make or break your success?*

TEACH LISTEN UP! Learning to resolve conflict in the workplace can mean the difference between success and failure. Communication is necessary for any lasting resolution of conflict and is combined with one of three strategies:

- **Collaborate** You and the other person work together toward a common goal.
- **Compromise** You and the other person both get some, but not all, of what you want.
- **Sacrifice** You let this one go and give the other person what he or she wants.

Tell students that the first two strategies are usually the best because they are both win/win, but with the third strategy, someone might come away angry.

LET'S EXPLORE The class describes conflicts they have experienced at work, home, or school.

- Write a 3-column chart on the board with these headings: Conflict, Method of Resolution, Other Possible Ways to Resolve.
- Write students' ideas in the first two columns. As a class, brainstorm other ways that the conflict could have been resolved. Add these to the third column.
- Discuss all of the options to decide what the best way to resolve each might have been.

TIME FOR Q & A Discover more about conflict resolution.

▶ *Why can't every conflict end with collaboration?*
Example: Sometimes the two goals prevent each other from happening.

▶ *What should you do if you can't resolve a conflict?*
Example: You may need to ask your manager to step in to make a decision about it.

REFLECT *Which conflict resolution strategy will you try first in future conflicts? Why?*

LESSON OBJECTIVE
Resolve conflicts at work using various strategies.

TERMS TO KNOW
collaborate: to work jointly with others toward a common goal
compromise: to choose something in between two different possibilities
resolution: the end of or answer to a problem
sacrifice: to let go of something you want for the sake of someone or something else

GOES WELL WITH LESSONS: 15, 54, 77

21st Century Activities ... Each done in under 21 minutes

PRACTICE
Making Sacrifices
Two employees both want the cubicle that has just opened up because it's near a window. Ask the class to brainstorm ways to resolve the conflict.
- Discuss possible ways they could collaborate.
- Discuss possible ways they could compromise.
- Discuss whether sacrifice is the only way to resolve the conflict.

Point out that both parties cannot get what they want and that compromise (for example, one person taking the cubicle and then the other) is probably not practical. Sacrifice is probably the only option.

☐ CLASS WORK ☐ HOMEWORK
☐ EXTRA CREDIT ☐ PROJECT

APPLY
Let's Work It Out
Individuals complete **Activity Sheet 95**.
- Read aloud the description of a workplace conflict resolution.
- For *Classify*, students read and then answer the questions.
- In their **Journal (p. W3)**, students reflect on a recent conflict resolution.

Possible Answers 1. Collaboration. **2.** Both people worked together to find a resolution.
EVALUATE: Answers will vary.

☐ CLASS WORK ☐ HOMEWORK
☐ EXTRA CREDIT ☐ PROJECT

EXTEND
Connect to Global Awareness
Conflict resolution between countries has even more of an impact than that between coworkers, but the same strategies can be used.

With a partner, choose an international conflict that is in the news. Research the reasons for the conflict and then briefly describe what collaboration, compromise, and sacrifice might each look like in a resolution for the conflict. Present your ideas to the class or on the class's Web page.

☐ CLASS WORK ☐ HOMEWORK
☐ EXTRA CREDIT ☐ PROJECT

Unit 2 Career Skills 45

NAME _____ DATE _____

Let's Work It Out

95 WHY TRY? Because— Ending conflicts helps everyone

INVESTIGATE Review the ways to end conflicts in the workplace. Then, read about a workplace conflict resolved through compromise

Usually conflicts can be resolved in one of three ways:

1. **Collaboration:** Both work together toward a common goal.
2. **Compromise:** Each person gets some, but not all, of what he or she wants.
3. **Sacrifice:** Only one person gets what he or she wants.

Kai was frustrated. He needed more overtime. He told his boss he needed it. But when his boss offered extra shifts, Kai always seemed to be gone from the shipping room, driving his route. His coworker Nolan got the work every time.

Kai talked to Nolan about it. Nolan said that he needed the overtime, too. He did not want to give it up. Kai pointed out that Nolan had the last four overtime shifts in a row. "I'm not looking for four in a row. I would just like to start trading back and forth." Nolan agreed.

CLASSIFY Read about another conflict. Then answer the questions.

Shom and Nesheba were having a tough time getting together to finish their report. Shom's family counted on him in the evening, and Nesheba had a part-time job in the evenings. They never had the same night free. Both of them were frustrated.

The report was due next Tuesday. So Shom went to Nesheba's cubicle.

"It's never fun to work weekends, and I know we've both been trying to avoid it. But if you're willing to work Saturday, I am, too."

Nesheba looked relieved. "I'm willing! Let's meet at 9:00 Saturday morning at the library. Maybe we can finish before noon and still get some time off."

"That sounds great," Shom said.

---

1. In which of the three ways was this conflict resolved? _____

2. Why do you think so? _____

_____

EVALUATE In your Journal, write about your last conflict at work, home, or school. How you resolve it? Were you happy with the results?

46   Lesson 95 Resolving Conflicts at Work   © 2011 Saddleback Educational Publishing

Being Truthful in Business

96

INTRODUCE **THINK ABOUT IT** *Is honesty the best policy when you are at work? Explain what you think and why.*

TEACH **LISTEN UP!** When people at work trust you to be **ethical** and tell the truth, supervisors and coworkers trust you. Being truthful means that you:

- Own up to your mistakes.
- Don't blame others.
- Tell the truth.
- Don't make promises you can't keep.

Point out that being honest is sometimes difficult or uncomfortable at work. Many people don't like to admit they made a mistake. Also, many people do not want to report coworkers who are dishonest or behave badly. However, it is important to be honest and straightforward at work so that people learn to trust you.

LET'S EXPLORE As a class, brainstorm work situations in which it might be difficult to discuss one's own mistakes or the mistakes of coworkers.

- Describe the situations in key words on the board.
- Discuss why it might be difficult to talk to managers about the problems.
- Discuss ways to be honest and straightforward in appropriate ways.

PLAY THESE ROLES Partners choose one of the situations the class discussed. Partners then select parts and role-play the situation. To assess students' understanding, observe role-plays. When necessary, model how to be honest and ethical in the situation.

REFLECT *What benefits might you get from being honest at work? In school?*

BEING TRUTHFUL IN BUSINESS

LESSON OBJECTIVE
Apply basic rules of honesty to work situations.

TERMS TO KNOW
ethical: following rules or principles of right and wrong behavior

GOES WELL WITH LESSONS:
25, 45, 96

21st Century Activities ... Each done in under 21 minutes

PRACTICE
It's How You Say It
Students discuss how to be tactful when being honest.
- On the board, write sentences with accusatory tones; e.g., *John is a liar. John didn't do his work because he wasted time gossiping with his coworkers. John is lazy.*
- Model how to restate one of the sentences; e.g., *Maybe John didn't tell the whole truth.*
- Groups revise the sentences.
- Volunteers present revisions to the class.

☐ CLASS WORK   ☐ HOMEWORK
☐ EXTRA CREDIT   ☐ PROJECT

APPLY
Handle a Work Situation
Pairs complete **Activity Sheet 96.**
- Students read the situation.
- Pairs write outcomes of ways to handle the situation.
- Pairs choose the best way.

Possible Answers 1. Ignoring the situation won't solve the problem or stop the salesperson from being dishonest again. **2.** Discussing it with the boss might get the salesperson in trouble but will help solve the problem. **3.** Complaining to coworkers won't solve the problem and will make me look bad. *CHOOSE:* Answers will vary.

☐ CLASS WORK   ☐ HOMEWORK
☐ EXTRA CREDIT   ☐ PROJECT

EXTEND
Connect to Business Literacy
Imagine that you are the owner of a business. What "honesty is the best policy" rules do you want your employees to follow?

Brainstorm a list of at least five rules. For each rule, give a rationale, or reason. For example, you might say, *If you make a big mistake, please let your supervisor know. That way, you can both figure out how to fix it.* Present your list of rules and reasons to the class.

☐ CLASS WORK   ☐ HOMEWORK
☐ EXTRA CREDIT   ☐ PROJECT

Unit 2 Career Skills

NAME _____ DATE _____

Handle a Work Situation

96 WHY TRY? Because— Honesty earns you trust!

INVESTIGATE Read the situation below.

What Should I Do?

You work in the office of a furniture store. Your job is to fill customers' orders. You get the orders from the store's salespeople. Then you place the orders with the store's warehouse. You like your job. But one of the salespeople makes your job harder. He makes promises that are hard to keep. This morning, he told a customer the store could deliver a new couch to her in two days. You know that's impossible. It will take five days just to get the couch from the warehouse to the store. How should you handle the situation?

DISCUSS Here are three ways you might handle the situation:

- Ignore it.
- Discuss it honestly with your boss.
- Discuss it honestly with your coworkers. Complain about what the salesman did.

With a partner, discuss the possible outcomes of each way. Write your ideas on the lines below.

1. If I ignore the situation, then . . .
_____
_____

2. If I discuss the situation honestly with my boss, then . . .
_____
_____

3. If I discuss the situation honestly with my coworkers, then . . .
_____
_____

CHOOSE Use the outcomes to make a choice. In your Journal, tell which way you would handle the situation and why.

Lesson 96 Being Truthful in Business

Reflecting on Your Work

97

REFLECTING ON YOUR WORK

INTRODUCE THINK ABOUT IT *How might reflecting on your work help you improve?*

TEACH LISTEN UP! When people **reflect** on their work, they **evaluate** whether their efforts are effective and how they can improve their work. By learning from the past to shape the future, people progress toward their goals. To reflect on your work, use an **inventory**, or questionnaire, to guide your thoughts. Consider these questions:

- Did I reach my goal?
- What worked and should be repeated?
- What didn't work? How can I improve that part?
- What information did I need that I did not have?
- How can I get missing information the next time?

LET'S EXPLORE Use an inventory to reflect on a recent class project.

- Review the project to make it fresh in students' mind.
- Discuss each of the five questions on the inventory, modeling how to reflect in a way that will help students do better work on future projects.

TIME FOR Q & A Discover how reflection can improve your work.

▸ **Describe a mistake you've repeated.**
I wait too long to start my work.

▸ **What should you do differently?**
start earlier; plan my time better

▸ **How can you do it differently?**
make and follow a schedule

▸ **How can you tell the plan works?**
by seeing if my work improves

REFLECT *How might reflection help you improve in one of your classes?*

LESSON OBJECTIVE
Use an inventory to reflect on work and ways to improve it.

TERMS TO KNOW
evaluate: to judge strengths and weaknesses
inventory: an itemized list
reflect: to think deeply about

GOES WELL WITH LESSONS:
5, 40, 106

21st Century Activities ... Each done in under 21 minutes

PRACTICE
Studying Your Study Habits
Students reflect on their study habits.
- Ask students to write answers to these questions:
- *Where do you study? Is the place quiet? Organized?*
- *How do you study? Are some methods more effective than others? Which ones work best?*
- *Recall a time you met a goal at school. How did you meet it? How can you repeat the success?*

☐ CLASS WORK ☐ HOMEWORK
☐ EXTRA CREDIT ☐ PROJECT

APPLY
The Mirror in Your Mind
Individuals complete **Activity Sheet 97**.
- Students read the reflection inventory.
- Students answer the inventory questions.
- Students make an action plan.

Possible Answers *APPLY:* Students' answers will vary but should be complete and show an understanding of how to reflect on work. *SYNTHESIZE:* Students' plans will vary but should be specific and should address strengths and weaknesses uncovered by reflecting.

☐ CLASS WORK ☐ HOMEWORK
☐ EXTRA CREDIT ☐ PROJECT

EXTEND
Connect to Environmental Literacy
We can all do our part to take care of our planet, even if we take only small, simple steps, like cutting back on waste, recycling, and using less paper. Reflect on ways you do—or do not—do your part.

Imagine that your goal is to help save the environment. What have you done in the past week to meet that goal? On a separate sheet of paper, answer the five reflection questions. Then list ways you can improve.

☐ CLASS WORK ☐ HOMEWORK
☐ EXTRA CREDIT ☐ PROJECT

Unit 2 Career Skills   49

NAME _____ DATE _____

The Mirror in Your Mind

97 WHY TRY? Because— Reflection helps me improve.

INVESTIGATE Read about why to reflect and how to do it.

When you reflect on your work, you evaluate how effective you have been. You also think of ways to improve. One way to reflect is to use a list of questions to answer:

- Did I reach my goal?
- What worked and should be repeated?
- What didn't work? How can I improve that part?
- What information did I need to have that I did not have?
- How can I get missing information next time?

APPLY Think about a project you did for a class or a job. To reflect on your work, answer these questions.

1. What was the project? _____
_____

2. Did I reach my goal? _____
_____

3. What worked and should be repeated? _____
_____

4. What didn't work? How can I improve that part? _____
_____

5. What information did I need that I didn't have? _____
_____

6. How could I get the information next time? _____

SYNTHESIZE Think about your answers to the questions. Then write an action plan for improving your work in one of your classes.

_____
_____
_____

Lesson 97 Reflecting on Your Work © 2011 Saddleback Educational Publishing

Communicating at Home, School, and Work

98

INTRODUCE **THINK ABOUT IT** *Why is good communication important?*

TEACH **LISTEN UP! Communication** can sometimes be uncomfortable. It might seem as if being heard is more important than listening. But if you truly listen, others are more likely to hear what you say. When you face an uncomfortable conversation:
- Think about what you are going to say—beforehand, if possible.
- Show respect. Don't interrupt, and be polite.
- Remember the difference between fact and opinion. This makes room for other people's different views of a situation.
- Listen carefully. Repeat what the other person says to make sure you understand. Ask questions about anything you do not understand.

LET'S EXPLORE As a class, think of a way that a teenager can approach her parents to ask for a later curfew. Help students think of ideas that match each of the steps listed above. Use the questions below to guide the students. Write their ideas on the board and discuss positive and negative ways to communicate.
- What could she practice saying?
- How can she show respect?
- How can she remember the difference between fact and opinion?
- How can she show her parents that she is listening?

PLAY THESE ROLES Kate, a server in a restaurant, talks with her coworker because she thinks he does not do enough of the cleaning.

REFLECT *Are you a good listener?*

COMMUNICATING AT HOME, SCHOOL, AND WORK

LESSON OBJECTIVE
Effectively communicate with people at home, school, and work using a variety of strategies.

TERMS TO KNOW
communication: the sharing of information
fact: something that can be proven to be true
opinion: a person's belief about something, that may or may not be true
respect: a sense of somebody else's worth

GOES WELL WITH LESSONS:
26, 55, 99

21st Century Activities ... Each done in under 21 minutes

PRACTICE
Communication Demonstration
Small groups develop a scene in which a boy tells his dad he's dented the car.
- The boy practices what he will say to his father.
- The boy speaks very respectfully.
- The boy gives his father the facts and then his opinion.
- The boy listens to everything his father says and then repeats it back to show he listened.

Help groups explore what might have happened if the boy had waited to tell his father until after his father discovered the dent.

☐ CLASS WORK ☐ HOMEWORK
☐ EXTRA CREDIT ☐ PROJECT

APPLY
Give and Take
Individuals complete **Activity Sheet 98**.
- Review communication steps, and then read the communication scenarios.
- Follow the directions for each item in *Analyze*.
- In the **Journal (p. W3)**, respond to *Write*.

Possible Answers 1–2. Answers will vary.
3. Facts: 3rd sentence; Opinions: first 2 sentences. **WRITE:** Answers will vary but should show an understanding of positive communication techniques.

☐ CLASS WORK ☐ HOMEWORK
☐ EXTRA CREDIT ☐ PROJECT

EXTEND
Connect to Global Awareness
English is a main language used to communicate internationally. However, many countries have different customs and ways to communicate.

With a partner, select a country and research methods of communication—oral, written, or nonverbal—that are preferred in that country. For example, it is important not to point your finger when you speak in China because it is offensive there. (Body language is a form of communication, too!) Choose three cultural elements to present to the class.

☐ CLASS WORK ☐ HOMEWORK
☐ EXTRA CREDIT ☐ PROJECT

Unit 3 People Skills   51

NAME _____ DATE _____

Give and Take

98 WHY TRY? Because— Good communicators avoid conflicts!

INVESTIGATE Review the important steps to take when communicating with others. Then, read the descriptions of communication scenarios at home, school, and work.

- Think about what you are going to say—beforehand, if possible.
- Show **respect.** Don't interrupt, and be polite.
- Remember the difference between **fact** and **opinion.** This makes room for other people's different views of a situation.
- Listen carefully. Repeat what the other person says to make sure you understand. Ask questions about anything you do not understand.

Home: You talk with your mom about missing an important family event on Friday night so that you can work a double shift.

School: Your teacher says, "I would like you to come in at the end of the school day so that we can talk about your last test. I think you misunderstood something that we can clear up pretty quickly."

Work: Your coworker, Ray, says that his boss, Joseph, is unfair and always gives Susan the best shifts. Ray says that Joseph doesn't have any confidence in Ray. Ray says that he has had only four shifts in two weeks.

ANALYZE Follow the directions for each item below.

1. In the **Home** scenario, you might want to practice what you want to say before having the conversation with your mom. Write what you would say to bring the subject up respectfully and to explain your wishes. _____
_____
_____

2. In the **School** scenario, your teacher's message is pretty vague and could be confusing. What questions would you ask him? _____
_____

3. In the **Work** scenario, your coworker gives you both facts and opinions. Underline the facts and circle the opinions in the scenario.

WRITE Think of something you have always wanted to do but haven't yet asked a parent or guardian about doing. In your Journal, write notes about what you would say to that person in order to be able to do it, including facts, if possible. Also write two possible objections your parent or guardian might have and ways you will respond to those objections.

Lesson 98 Communicating at Home, School, and Work © 2011 Saddleback Educational Publishing

Listening Effectively

INTRODUCE **THINK ABOUT IT** *Are you an effective listener?*

TEACH **LISTEN UP!** **Active listening** can help you remember information spoken aloud:
- **Get rid of distractions** by turning off music or cell phones.
- **Ask questions** when the time is right. Wait until a pause in the conversation.
- **Take notes** on what you hear. Writing down the important parts of a speaker's message will help you remember the information and give you a chance to review it.

Tell students that they can use a technique like the one below to improve their listening skills.

Repeat	Restate	Write
Say a sentence using the speaker's words: *"Timeliness is very important."*	Say the speaker's words in similar language: *"Being on time is very important."*	Write the speaker's meaning in your own words: *"Don't be late!"*

LET'S EXPLORE Students listen actively to directions to a local park, mall, or theater.
- Encourage students to ask questions for details or clarification.
- Have students repeat, restate, and write key phrases or details.

THINK, PAIR, SHARE Have pairs take turns describing a recent sports event or movie they have seen. First, listeners ask questions and restate phrases in their own words to clarify meaning. Then, have the speakers say the description again, while the listeners take notes.

REFLECT *What are some ways you can become a better listener?*

99 LISTENING EFFECTIVELY

LESSON OBJECTIVE
Listen effectively in order to understand spoken information.

TERMS TO KNOW
active listening: a method of listening carefully and asking questions to improve understanding
distractions: things that take away from focus

GOES WELL WITH LESSONS:
21, 43, 76

21st Century Activities ... Each done in under 21 minutes

PRACTICE
Listening Game
Students form a line. The student on one end whispers a three- to five-line story to the next student. Each student will recall and retell the story to the next student in the line.
- Tell students that they will hear the story only once, but that they may whisper one question for clarification.
- When the story reaches the end of the line, have the final student say it aloud and compare it to the original story.
- Reorder the students in the line and do the activity again with a new story.

☐ CLASS WORK ☐ HOMEWORK
☐ EXTRA CREDIT ☐ PROJECT

APPLY
Listen Effectively
Individuals complete **Activity Sheet 99**.
- Students complete the Repeat, Restate, and Write flow chart.
- Students read the paragraph aloud and rate their listening effectiveness.
- Students read aloud again. The listening partner summarizes in his or her own words in the **Journal (p. W3)**.

Possible Answers INVESTIGATE:
Restate People who water their lawns on unscheduled days will have to pay money.
Write People can only water their lawns on scheduled days. *REMEMBER:* Answers will vary.

☐ CLASS WORK ☐ HOMEWORK
☐ EXTRA CREDIT ☐ PROJECT

EXTEND
Connect to Civic Literacy
When someone runs for public office, that person gives speeches to tell people why they should vote for him or her. Voters need to listen actively to candidates' messages.

Pretend you are running for President. Write a short speech to explain why you would be good at the job. Then read your speech aloud to your partner, who actively listens and takes notes. In turn, you listen and take notes as your partner reads his or her speech aloud. Compare your notes.

☐ CLASS WORK ☐ HOMEWORK
☐ EXTRA CREDIT ☐ PROJECT

Unit 3 People Skills

NAME _____ DATE _____

Listen Effectively

99 WHY TRY? Because— Active listening helps me understand!

INVESTIGATE Find out how to listen effectively.

Active listening is a strategy to improve the way you listen and to help you better understand what you hear. You can listen actively when you:

- Get rid of **distractions**.
- Ask questions.
- Take notes.
- Use the Repeat, Restate, and Write technique.

Read the following example to a partner and then complete the Repeat, Restate, and Write.

Original statement: *The new rules for water usage go into effect in May, and there will be fines for homeowners who water lawns on unscheduled days.*

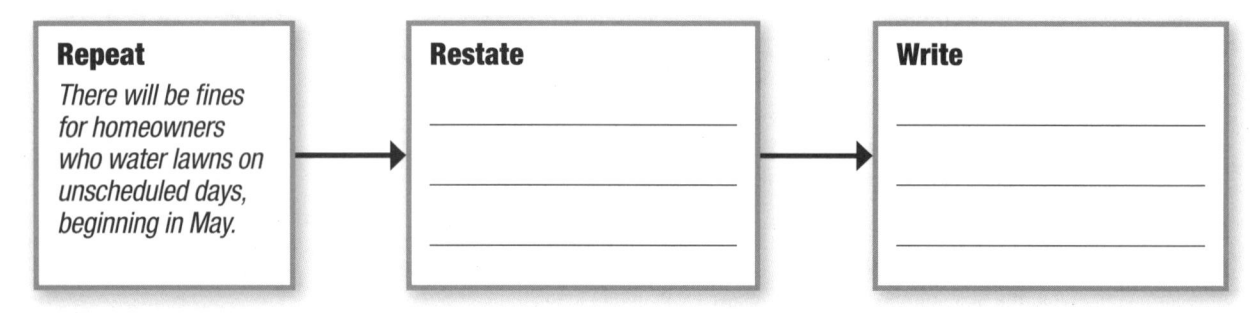

Repeat	Restate	Write
There will be fines for homeowners who water lawns on unscheduled days, beginning in May.		

REMEMBER Listen to your partner read this paragraph aloud. Do not follow along by reading the words while he or she is reading aloud. Cover the paragraph with a piece of paper, if necessary.

> The Living History project will take six weeks of preparation. During this time, students read about a famous historical character and create a costume for the character. When they are finished, students wear the costume and present facts about the character's life.

After your partner is finished reading, circle Yes or No to rate your Listening Effectiveness.

1. **Yes | No** Was I distracted by other things while I listened?
2. **Yes | No** Did I think of questions that would help me better understand the speaker?
3. **Yes | No** Can I repeat the important parts of the speaker's information?
4. **Yes | No** Can I restate the speaker's message in simpler words?

APPLY Listen to your partner read the paragraph one more time. This time, take notes on what you hear. In your Journal, restate the information in your own words.

Collaborating at Work

100

COLLABORATING AT WORK

INTRODUCE **THINK ABOUT IT** *Think about a time you worked with a group on a project or other task. Was the experience good or bad? Why?*

TEACH **LISTEN UP!** When people work as a team, every team member should contribute in some way. In order for a team to get the best results, they should **collaborate**. Team members should:

- **contribute** to the team by paying attention and sharing ideas.
- respect one another's differences and opinions.
- listen to others and not **dominate** the discussion.
- find a way to **compromise** when there are differences of opinion.

Tell students: *A group is not collaborating if only one member does all the work. A successful team finds a way to divide tasks and still meet its goals and deadlines.*

LET'S EXPLORE Discuss how a team could help a bakery develop a new product.

- As a class, spend three minutes brainstorming types of products that might be successful, such as holiday-themed bakery items.
- Discuss different approaches and ideas. Encourage suggestions from as many class members as possible.
- Ask class members to identify the types of tasks needed to create this new product.

TIME FOR Q & A Discover what can happens when teams collaborate.

▸ *What is the team's main goal and deadline?* To create a healthy or a popular product in time for the holiday rush

▸ *How can everyone contribute?* All team members offer ideas and work on their assigned tasks.

REFLECT *What kinds of people make up the best teams?*

LESSON OBJECTIVE
Collaborate to work effectively as a group.

TERMS TO KNOW
collaborate: to work with one or more people on a project
compromise: to come to an agreement
contribute: to provide or give
dominate: to control

GOES WELL WITH LESSONS:
34, 48, 74

21st Century Activities ... Each done in under **21** minutes

PRACTICE
Collaborate on a Story
Students pretend they are part of a writing team at a publishing company. Their task is to collaborate to write a story that the company will publish.
- One student offers a story starter, such as "Once upon a time."
- The next student then offers a few lines of the story, then the next student, and so on.
- One student writes down the story in the order in which it's told.
- Students then reread their story and collaborate by offering suggestions to make it better. Groups read their stories aloud in class.

☐ CLASS WORK ☐ HOMEWORK
☐ EXTRA CREDIT ☐ PROJECT

APPLY
Let's Collaborate!
Small groups complete **Activity Sheet 100**.
- Students read, then answer the *Analyze* questions.
- Students collaborate as a group to come up with ideas to improve the health club team's collaboration.

Possible Answers 1. Only two team members contributed ideas. **2.** Team members did not respect the member who wanted to ask for other opinions. **3.** Team members did not compromise. One opinion dominated. **EVALUATE:** Answers will vary, but should include that the team get other opinions.

☐ CLASS WORK ☐ HOMEWORK
☐ EXTRA CREDIT ☐ PROJECT

EXTEND
Connect to Civic Literacy
Consider how often people work together in a school, neighborhood, or community to complete projects. Often, groups of workplace volunteers do jobs that are too large to be done by individuals.

Work in small groups to choose a project that could be done in our community, such as making an urban garden or building a new playground. As a team, collaborate to set goals and assign tasks. After the team has completed its plan, make a poster that shows the proposal for your community improvement project.

☐ CLASS WORK ☐ HOMEWORK
☐ EXTRA CREDIT ☐ PROJECT

Unit 3 People Skills

NAME _____ DATE _____

Let's Collaborate!

100 WHY TRY? Because— Teamwork gets a job done!

INVESTIGATE When a team of people collaborate, they work together on a single project. Collaboration works best when a team follows rules. On a successful workplace team, everyone should:

- **contribute** to the team.
- respect one another.
- listen carefully to others.
- **compromise.**

ANALYZE Read the description below. Then answer the questions to analyze the strengths and weaknesses of the team's collaboration.

> Five employees at a health club met to talk about adding more fitness classes to the club's schedule. All the employees were from the business office. One said that the health club would make more money if it added five new classes. One person said that he would like to ask a yoga instructor about the new classes, but all the other members argued that instructors were too busy to go to meetings. They also argued that if the health club could make more money, they should just set up the five classes.

1. How well did all the members of the team contribute to the meeting?

_____
_____

2. Did group members respect one another's opinions? Explain.

_____
_____

3. Did team members dominate the discussion, or did they listen and compromise?

_____
_____

EVALUATE With a small group, offer suggestions for improving the team described in the exercise above. Write the group's ideas in your Journal. Then, choose one group member to present the ideas to the class.

56 Lesson 100 Collaborating at Work © 2011 Saddleback Educational Publishing

Influencing People

101

INFLUENCING PEOPLE

INTRODUCE THINK ABOUT IT *What are the best ways to influence people and help them believe your ideas are good ones?*

TEACH LISTEN UP! When you **influence** people, you persuade them that your idea is a good one. The way you decide to persuade people depends on your situation. You might:

- **Convince** people that your idea helps them reach their own goals.
- Recognize others' point of view and show respect for their ideas.
- Reach out to people by **blending** their ideas with your own.

Tell students that they probably will not influence others by making demands. It is more effective to talk to people calmly and help them understand that your idea is reasonable, helpful, and smart.

LET'S EXPLORE Brainstorm ways to make a persuasive argument for improving the school cafeteria.

- Have the class spend 1–5 minutes brainstorming ideas for cafeteria improvements.
- Select three ideas for discussion.
- Point out possible objections to the ideas.
- Have the class discuss persuasive ways to overcome the objections.

TIME FOR Q & A Practice persuading people who might not agree with your ideas. For Q & A, select one of the ideas from the list you created in *Let's Explore*.

▶ *What if people say your idea is too expensive?*
Research your idea and show its actual cost. To persuade, you could explain how you hope to pay for your idea.

▶ *What if people like things the way they are?*
Example: Blend ideas. Ask people what they like best about the system, and make sure those things don't change.

REFLECT *What could happen if you do not respect others' ideas?*

LESSON OBJECTIVE
Apply people skills to exert a positive influence on teammates.

TERMS TO KNOW
blending: putting together or combining
convince: to make someone believe something
influence: to persuade or convince

GOES WELL WITH LESSONS:
20, 51, 104

21st Century Activities ... Each done in under 21 minutes

PRACTICE
Cooperative Learning
Present groups of 3–4 with a set of statements. For example: *You should join the swim team* or *Our class t-shirts should be blue.* Then have the group discuss how it could influence others to agree.
- Groups practice presenting benefits of their ideas to others.
- Groups think of possible objections to the ideas and practice blending ideas to include others' input.

☐ CLASS WORK ☐ HOMEWORK
☐ EXTRA CREDIT ☐ PROJECT

APPLY
My Way or the Highway
Groups of 4–5 complete **Activity Sheet 101.**
- Students read the paragraph, answer questions 1–3, and act out the scene.
- Encourage creativity, humor, and natural-sounding language.
- Students answer *Analyze* questions in their **Journal (p. W3).**

Possible Answers 1. No. His idea seems silly and not useful. **2.** Frederick's, Skye's, and Lula's points are good. **3.** They don't like it. **4** & **5.** Answers will vary, but students should offer ideas that show teamwork and compromise.

☐ CLASS WORK ☐ HOMEWORK
☐ EXTRA CREDIT ☐ PROJECT

EXTEND
Connect to Environmental Literacy
Sometimes people do not like new ideas because they do not yet have enough information about them. For example, people may not want to compost or buy recycled products because they do not know how those activities can help the planet.

Think about a way our school could be more "green." Research your idea to learn how the change could help the environment and the community. Then make a persuasive **digital presentation** that uses facts to influence people to make this change.

☐ CLASS WORK ☐ HOMEWORK
☐ EXTRA CREDIT ☐ PROJECT

Unit 3 People Skills

NAME _____ DATE _____

My Way or the Highway

101 WHY TRY? Because— I can positively influence people!

INVESTIGATE ▶ Find out how to influence people.

When you **influence** friends or coworkers, you persuade them to see things your way. People may be persuaded if you show them how your idea helps them. They probably will not be persuaded if you do not consider their ideas and their point of view. One successful way of persuading people is to **blend**, or combine, ideas.

DRAMATIZE ▶ Read the description of the scene below. Then answer the questions to organize your thoughts about the scene. With a group, act out the scene to show an unsuccessful example of persuasion. Show what happens if a person tries to persuade by insisting on "my way."

My Way or the Highway

All the after-school clubs are asked to have a booth at the annual school open house. Jackson, the Chess Club president, tells the club that they will all dress up like giant chess pieces and play a game of chess during the open house. Lauren and Ellie object to wearing costumes. Frederick points out that they might not have space for a giant chess game. Skye and Lula suggest that they should be talking to new members and not playing chess. Jackson says, "My way or the highway," and he refuses to change.

---

1. Is Jackson's suggestion a good one? Why or why not?

_____

_____

2. Do the other members raise reasonable objections? Explain.

_____

_____

3. How do you think the other members feel about Jackson's response?

_____

_____

ANALYZE ▶ Review your presentation. Answer these questions in your Journal.

4. What could Jackson have said to be more persuasive?

5. Describe a blended idea that might have been more persuasive than Jackson's.

Lesson 101 Influencing People

Showing Integrity

102

SHOWING INTEGRITY

INTRODUCE THINK ABOUT IT *How do your actions show that you have integrity?*

TEACH LISTEN UP! Showing **integrity** means that we act according to values we say are important to us. When we have integrity, our actions back up our words to show our **character**. Having integrity means that our actions:

- Show our **honesty,** even when no one is looking.
- Indicate that we **respect** our school, community, and those around us.
- Show how we can put the needs of others ahead of our own.

Tell students that **integrity** comes from a root word that means "completeness." Having integrity means that if we say we believe in something, such as *honesty* or *loyalty,* then our actions always show that value.

LET'S EXPLORE As a class, brainstorm ways that people could show integrity.

- Spend 3 minutes making a list of the ways to show integrity, such as not parking in handicapped spaces or not cheating on a test when there's an opportunity to do so.
- Then brainstorm situations that might make it difficult to show integrity, even if you believed in a particular value, such as finding $100 and deciding whether to keep it or find its rightful owner.

TIME FOR Q & A Have students further explore how they show integrity in their daily actions.

▶ *How does picking up trash or recycling show your integrity?* It shows respect for the environment and the community.

▶ *How does following school rules show your integrity?* It shows that you respect other students and your teachers, and that you want to be a good, fair person.

REFLECT *How can you always act with fairness and integrity?*

LESSON OBJECTIVE
Identify and apply actions that show integrity and putting the needs of others ahead of your own.

TERMS TO KNOW
character: a person's values and moral qualities
honesty: truthfulness
integrity: the state of being ethical and honest
respect: to treat well and with honor

GOES WELL WITH LESSONS: 20, 56, 105

21st Century Activities ... Each done in under 21 minutes

PRACTICE
R-E-S-P-E-C-T!
Divide the class into two teams. Play a game about respect.

- Give students two **Note Cards** (p. W10). On one, they write a scene that describes a respectful action; on the other, a disrespectful action.
- One player from each team comes to the front of the class. You read one card from the shuffled deck.
- Players ring a **bell** to "buzz in" (as on a game show) to be the first to say whether the scene shows respect or disrespect. Then the next pair approach to play, and so on.

☐ CLASS WORK ☐ HOMEWORK
☐ EXTRA CREDIT ☐ PROJECT

APPLY
How Do Actions Show Integrity?
Individuals complete **Activity Sheet 102.**
- Students read, then respond to items 1–3, explaining why each choice shows integrity.
- In the **Journal (p. W3)** students write about a time they showed integrity.

Possible Answers 1. *B;* explaining the answer helps classmates learn it.
2. *A;* taking full credit would not be honest.
3. *B;* recycling shows respect for the environment. **WRITE:** Answers will vary based on personal experience.

☐ CLASS WORK ☐ HOMEWORK
☐ EXTRA CREDIT ☐ PROJECT

EXTEND
Connect to Global Awareness
Learning about other cultures is a way of showing our respect for them. We show integrity when we respect different customs because we show that we value our community and people's differences.

Learn more about a culture that you see in your school or community. Research that culture by interviewing an individual or by doing an Internet search. When you are done, bring back five facts about that culture to share with the class. Include a visual aid when you make your presentation.

☐ CLASS WORK ☐ HOMEWORK
☐ EXTRA CREDIT ☐ PROJECT

Unit 3 People Skills   59

NAME _____ DATE _____

102 WHY TRY? Because— I'm fair and honest!

How Do Actions Show Integrity?

INVESTIGATE Your everyday actions show people your values.

When we show **integrity,** we put the needs of others ahead of our own.

- When we follow the rules of a school or community, our actions show that we **respect** them.
- When we help others in our school or community, our actions show that we put the needs of others ahead of our own. Helping others shows **integrity**.

We can tell people what our values are, but the way we act shows our values much more clearly.

COMPARE Read the situations below. Then circle the letter of the action that shows integrity and explain how it does so.

1. Two classmates ask for help with a math problem. You:
   a. tell them the answer.
   b. show them how to do that type of problem.

This action shows integrity by: _____
_____

2. Your group did a project for science class. Your job was to summarize the experiment, but a teammate gave you helpful suggestions. When the teacher praises your summary, you:
   a. share credit with your teammate.
   b. say, "Thanks! I worked hard!"

This action shows integrity by: _____
_____

3. You drank a bottle of water at your school's track meet. There's no recycling bin on your side of the field, and many bottles are thrown on the ground. You:
   a. put your bottle with the others and write a letter to the school newspaper.
   b. walk to the other side of the field to recycle your bottle.

This action shows integrity by: _____
_____

WRITE In your Journal, write a paragraph about a time you showed integrity. What happened? How did your actions affect others? What might have happened if you hadn't shown integrity?

Lesson 102 Showing Integrity © 2011 Saddleback Educational Publishing

Being a Good Leader

103

BEING A GOOD LEADER

INTRODUCE THINK ABOUT IT *What makes a good leader? How do good leaders interact with a team?*

TEACH LISTEN UP! Good leaders help teammates use their strengths to help the team. A good leader can communicate well, solve problems, and help a team meet its goals. Often, this skill requires leaders to **adapt** their styles to the people they work with. The management style called "Up, Down, and Sideways" is one effective leadership style.

- **Leading Up:** leading by helping bosses or managers with a higher rank
- **Leading Down:** leading by helping staff, or **subordinates,** who rank below you
- **Leading Sideways:** leading by helping **peers,** or people of the same rank

Managers who "Lead Up" find ways to support their own managers and help them find solutions and information. People who "Lead Down" provide models for people on their team. Those who "Lead Sideways" help people in similar positions of responsibility work through problems together.

LET'S EXPLORE As a class, discuss strategies a manager could use to help subordinates who have not met their deadlines.

- Identify whether the manager would use an Up, Down, or Sideways leadership style.
- Write strategies on the board.
- Point out examples of leadership that improve communication and help the team.

THINK, PAIR, SHARE Have pairs discuss the strategies from the board. Ask volunteers to share their thoughts on why some strategies would be more effective than others.

REFLECT *What are ways that a good leader can help other workers do a better job?*

LESSON OBJECTIVE
Recognize different leadership styles and practice applying them.

TERMS TO KNOW
adapt: to change
subordinates: people with less authority or a lower rank than another person
peer: a person who is of equal standing in a group

GOES WELL WITH LESSONS: 35, 55, 95

21st Century Activities ... Each done in under 21 minutes

PRACTICE
Leadership Problem-Solving
Divide the class into teams that include the resident, manager, and associate of a business that makes and sells healthful food.

- Have each member of the group discuss how he or she will use the "Up, Down, and Sideways" management style.
- Ask each member to answer this question: *Whom can you help to lead? How can you be a good leader to these people?*
- Teams should present their findings to the class and discuss the opportunities for each type of employee to show leadership.

☐ CLASS WORK ☐ HOMEWORK
☐ EXTRA CREDIT ☐ PROJECT

APPLY
Which Way Do You Lead?
Groups of 3–4 complete **Activity Sheet 103.**
- Students read, then create a chart for *Apply.*
- For *Analyze,* students write in their **Journal (p. W3).**

Possible Answers APPLY: Up Suggest a rule to the owner of the company. **Down** Have your employees make good displays. **Sideways** Share your thoughts with other managers. **ANALYZE: 1.** Leading Sideways would be best, because then all the managers would follow the same rule. **2.** You could Lead Sideways by gathering information and sharing the results.

☐ CLASS WORK ☐ HOMEWORK
☐ EXTRA CREDIT ☐ PROJECT

EXTEND
Connect to Health Literacy
Sometimes, you need a leader to set a good example for others. A good leader in a school can show peers, younger students, and teachers how to make good choices about healthful living.

Find an article about children's health in a recent print or online newspaper. Read it to find information about nutrition and exercise for children. Use the information to make a presentation about how kids in school could Lead Up, Lead Down, and Lead Sideways to improve the overall health of students and staff in your school.

☐ CLASS WORK ☐ HOMEWORK
☐ EXTRA CREDIT ☐ PROJECT

Unit 3 People Skills

NAME _____ DATE _____

Which Way Do You Lead?

103 WHY TRY? Because— I can lead others to success!

INVESTIGATE Good leaders adapt their styles for different situations.

"Leading Up": Providing bosses with problem-solving suggestions.

"Leading Down": Being a role model for people you supervise.

"Leading Sideways": Building relationships and providing support to **peers.**

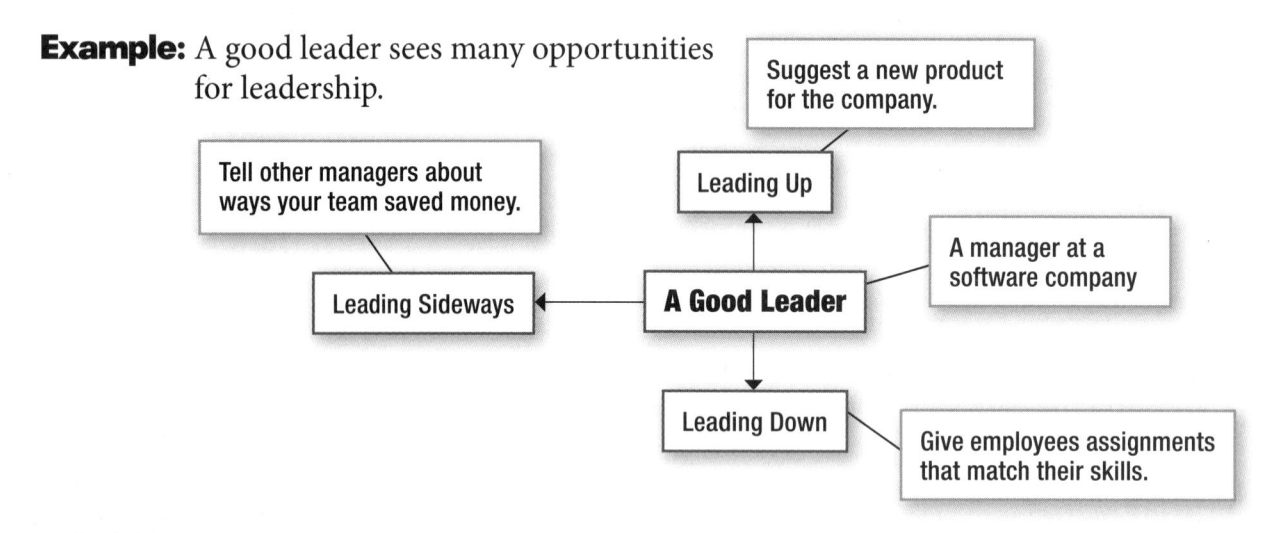

Example: A good leader sees many opportunities for leadership.

- Suggest a new product for the company. → **Leading Up**
- A manager at a software company → **A Good Leader**
- Tell other managers about ways your team saved money. → **Leading Sideways**
- Give employees assignments that match their skills. → **Leading Down**

APPLY Read this paragraph. Then chart examples of how to Lead Up, Down, and Sideways.

> You are a manager in one area of a big electronics store. Workers in many areas of your store disagree about how to display items. Some workers want to show as many items as possible. Other workers do not. You notice that customers have a hard time finding items when the display is cluttered. How can you use this information to Lead Up, Down, and Sideways?

EVALUATE Answer the questions in your Journal.

1. In the example above, would it be most effective to Lead Up, Down, or Sideways? Why?
2. In the example above, how can you Lead Sideways get your peers to solve the problem?

62   Lesson 103 Being a Good Leader   © 2011 Saddleback Educational Publishing

Being a Team Player

104

BEING A TEAM PLAYER

INTRODUCE THINK ABOUT IT *Why is it important to be a team player? What are the advantages of a team?*

TEACH LISTEN UP! Being a team player assumes that teamwork has benefits—if you work with other people, you can do more work in less time. You also have more brains to solve a problem. However, teamwork benefits its members only if they follow some rules:
- Everyone **participates**—that means all the team members have a job to do.
- Team members take turns—no one **dominates** a conversation or insists on an idea. A team **compromise** works much better than team disagreement.
- A team succeeds if its members can listen to each other and get along. When the group **cooperates,** it gets more work done.

Ask: *What qualities are important for being a team player?* Help students understand that communication and respect for one another's ideas help team members work well together.

LET'S EXPLORE Brainstorm ideas about how members of a team working on a project could solve a problem.
- Review the rules of teamwork.
- Spend three minutes gathering ideas.
- Point out opportunities for a team to use new ideas or compromise to solve its problem. Emphasize that all members of a team need to contribute to problem solving.

THINK, PAIR, SHARE Have pairs discuss experiences they have had in working on team projects. Ask them to share examples of good teamwork and suggestions for improvement.

REFLECT *What could you do to be a great team player?*

LESSON OBJECTIVE
Follow teamwork rules to work effectively in a group.

TERMS TO KNOW
compromise: a decision in which each person or group gives up something to reach an agreement
cooperate: to work together for a common goal
dominate: to take over
participate: to take part in

GOES WELL WITH LESSONS: 34, 55, 74

21st Century Activities ... Each done in under 21 minutes

PRACTICE
Make Team Assignments
Small groups plan how to divide jobs among team members.
- Chose a project, such as a poster or a multimedia presentation.
- Groups determine what tasks will be required to make the product, such as researching, writing, or illustrating.
- Team members discuss the tasks and assign jobs to each member.
- Have groups evaluate their decisions and explain how they benefited the project.

Suggest that teams think about how long each task might take. In addition, they can consider the special skills or interests of the team members.

☐ CLASS WORK ☐ HOMEWORK
☐ EXTRA CREDIT ☐ PROJECT

APPLY
Who's On My Team?
Groups of 2–3 complete **Activity Sheet 104.**
- Students read *Investigate* and discuss the rules of teamwork.
- Students read *Evaluate* and answer questions 1–3.
- Students answer the *Create* question in the **Journal (p. W3).**

Possible Answers 1. Hector and Frances could communicate to answer questions. **2.** Marissa broke the rule about participation. **3.** Josh could have started earlier or asked teammates for help. **4.** Maddie and Jesus might suggest that team members provide e-mail addresses and phone numbers to work together.

☐ CLASS WORK ☐ HOMEWORK
☐ EXTRA CREDIT ☐ PROJECT

EXTEND
Connect to Business Literacy
New businesses often change and adapt their products to increase sales and improve their profits. For example, a bike shop might order different bikes, depending on what its customers liked or did not like. Businesses often have teams of employees work together to decide on and make changes.

As a team, think about a product that you like but that you think could be improved. Draw or explain the features that you would like to see changed. Present your improved product with a computer-generated image or a simple model.

☐ CLASS WORK ☐ HOMEWORK
☐ EXTRA CREDIT ☐ PROJECT

Unit 3 People Skills

NAME _____ DATE _____

Who's on My Team?

104 WHY TRY? Because—Teamwork gets the job done!

INVESTIGATE Find out the rules of teamwork.

People on teams make certain agreements in order to work together effectively. First, everyone has to **participate**—no one can sit back and watch. Next, team members have to take turns and **cooperate** in order for a team to work together smoothly. Finally, teams can learn to **compromise** when necessary to reach an agreement.

EVALUATE Read the description below. Then answer the following questions to evaluate how well the team worked together.

> Six members of a history class were assigned a project about the Civil War. Maddie and Marissa were supposed to find information about a battle. Josh and Jesus were to find information about the Union army there. Hector and Frances were to report on the Confederate army. However, Marissa had to go out of town and couldn't do her research. Josh waited until the weekend to do his work and couldn't find his assignment on the school website. Hector and Frances used instant messages to talk about their research. Then they wrote their summary together. Maddie and Jesus ended up doing their work by themselves, since their partners couldn't help them.

1. Why were Hector and Frances able to work together to get their assignment done?
_____
_____

2. What rule about teamwork did Marissa break? _____
_____

3. How could Josh have been a better team player? _____
_____

DEVELOP Answer the question in your Journal.

4. What suggestions might Maddie and Jesus make about improving the teamwork process?
_____
_____

Lesson 104 Being a Team Player © 2011 Saddleback Educational Publishing

Embracing Differences

INTRODUCE **THINK ABOUT IT** *How do differences make our society stronger? Today we will find out how to better understand and value cultural differences.*

TEACH **LISTEN UP!** The people in the United States are culturally **diverse.** They are of different races, use different languages, and practice different customs. Learning about these differences in a school or workplace is important to

- prevent cultural misunderstandings
- avoid **stereotyping** or **bias**
- make decisions based on knowledge and understanding rather than guesswork

Tell students that people from different cultures and backgrounds may have different approaches to learning, communicating, and problem solving. Respecting these differences helps people to succeed in a **multicultural** society.

LET'S EXPLORE Name as many ways of greeting a person as you can.

- For 1–2 minutes, think of words, phrases, and gestures that communicate "hello."
- Write the ideas on the board.
- Point out that greetings may differ according to time and place. Ask: *Does a greeting change depending on who says it? Is it possible for "hello" to be misunderstood?*

TIME FOR Q & A Discover more about particular cultures and customs: Chinese National Day; Cinco de Mayo; Indian Diwali; Chuseok, the Korean Harvest Festival.

- ▸ **When is China's National Day celebrated?** October 1
- ▸ **What does Cinco de Mayo celebrate?** Mexican victory over the French in 1862
- ▸ **Whom does the Harvest Festival honor?** Korean ancestors
- ▸ **How long does Diwali last?** five days

REFLECT *Why is it important to learn about cultural differences?*

105

EMBRACING DIFFERENCES

LESSON OBJECTIVE
Understand and show respect for cultural and social differences.

TERMS TO KNOW
bias: an unfair judgment
diverse: different in culture, language, or race
multicultural: relating to many different cultures or societies
stereotyping: judging people based on their group, rather than their individual traits

GOES WELL WITH LESSONS: 15, 44, 77

21st Century Activities ... Each done in under 21 minutes

PRACTICE
What Do I Know About Them?
Post **pieces of newsprint** around the classroom with labels of different types of people or groups, for example, Teenagers, Wealthy People, Asian Americans, and Hispanic Americans.

- Have students circulate the room and write on the paper one thing that they "know" or have heard about the identified group.
- When students have written on each piece of paper, discuss how they know this information.
- Lead a discussion about how people learn stereotypes, and how to expand our thinking about people of different cultural groups.

☐ CLASS WORK ☐ HOMEWORK
☐ EXTRA CREDIT ☐ PROJECT

APPLY
What in the World Does That Mean?
Groups of 3–4 complete **Activity Sheet 105.**
- Students read the first box.
- Encourage multiple responses and points of view.

Possible Answers *UNDERSTAND:*
1. The partner may be showing respect. **2.** The silent person may be showing politeness. **3.** Some kids may not have money for T-shirts. *SYNTHESIZE:* Students may say they could bridge gaps by asking questions, showing patience, and listening carefully.

☐ CLASS WORK ☐ HOMEWORK
☐ EXTRA CREDIT ☐ PROJECT

EXTEND
Connect to Global Awareness
People from different parts of the nation and the world have their own sayings, actions, and manners that make their cultures rich and interesting.

Think about your own culture. What part of it might be confusing to a person from another state or country? Write down an example of one thing that is special to your culture—a custom, habit, or tradition. Then think about how you would explain it to someone from another country. Post the examples and explanations on a classroom map that shows where the customs originated.

☐ CLASS WORK ☐ HOMEWORK
☐ EXTRA CREDIT ☐ PROJECT

Unit 3 People Skills 65

NAME _____ DATE _____

What in the World Does That Mean?

105 WHY TRY? Because— Differences make us interesting!

INVESTIGATE Find out how to recognize and appreciate cultural differences.

People have different accents, depending on where they live. Similarly, they can have different customs and manners depending on their culture. Recognizing these differences helps us avoid misunderstandings and cultural clashes. Appreciating them means that you value the differences in your life.

UNDERSTAND Read the situations described below. Then fill out boxes to explain the cultural difference and suggest ways to bridge the cultural gap.

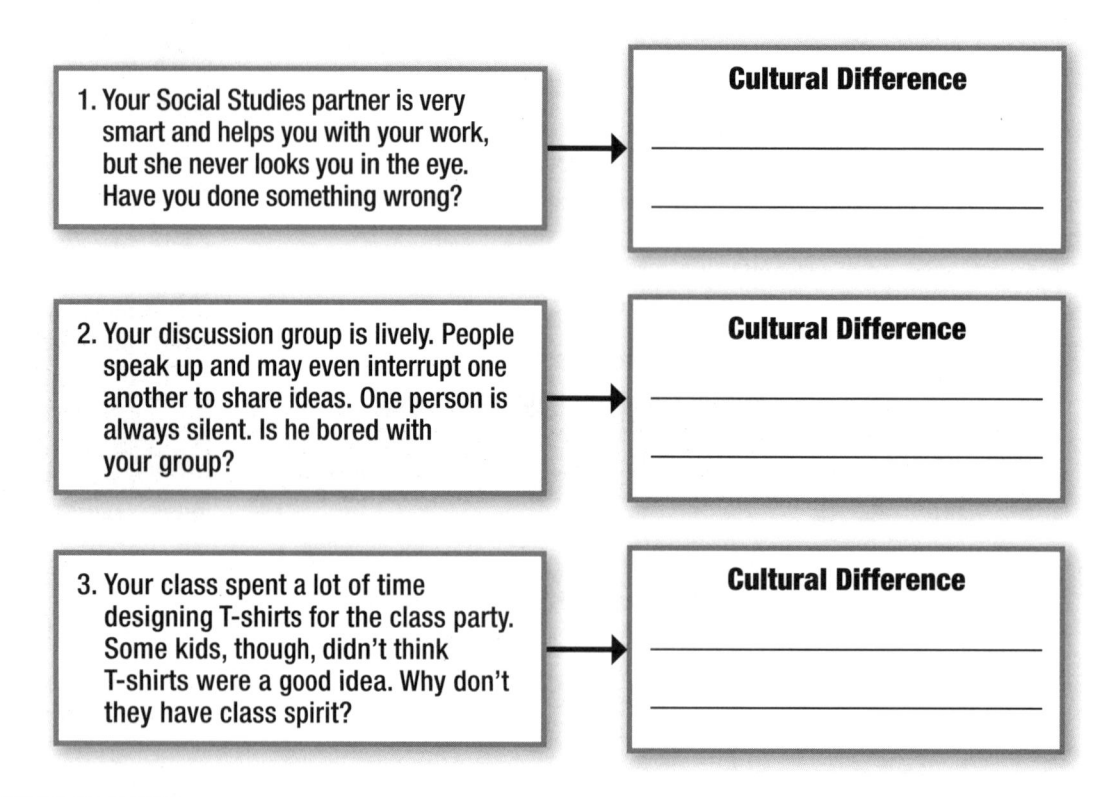

1. Your Social Studies partner is very smart and helps you with your work, but she never looks you in the eye. Have you done something wrong? → **Cultural Difference** _____

2. Your discussion group is lively. People speak up and may even interrupt one another to share ideas. One person is always silent. Is he bored with your group? → **Cultural Difference** _____

3. Your class spent a lot of time designing T-shirts for the class party. Some kids, though, didn't think T-shirts were a good idea. Why don't they have class spirit? → **Cultural Difference** _____

SYNTHESIZE After you identify the cultural difference in each box above, work in groups to brainstorm how to bridge this cultural gap. Post your ideas on a class bulletin board or Web site.

Lesson 105 Embracing Differences

Acting Responsibly

106
ACTING RESPONSIBLY

INTRODUCE THINK ABOUT IT *Are you a responsible person who can be trusted to do the right thing?*

TEACH LISTEN UP! People who are **responsible** do the right thing in any situation. People act responsibly when they:
- act in an **ethical** way, showing they can differentiate between right and wrong.
- act with **integrity**, showing they follow a set of **morals**.
- are trustworthy and keep their word.
- are good citizens who think of others, not just about themselves.

Acting responsibly means that you complete schoolwork on time or ask teachers for help. It also means that you do not act in a dishonest way. For example, you might be *popular* if you told friends the answers to a test, but you would not be *responsible*.

LET'S EXPLORE As a class, list times when students have acted responsibly.
- On the board, write students' examples from school, work, or home.
- Discuss what qualities made each action responsible and what might have happened if the action had not been responsible. For example: *If I hadn't acted responsibly when I babysat my younger brother, he could have gotten hurt.*

THINK, PAIR, SHARE Have pairs discuss the qualities they want in a good friend. Then have them compare those qualities to the examples listed on the board. Ask random pairs to share their thoughts on why good friends might be people who act responsibly.

REFLECT *How can acting responsibly help both yourself and others?*

LESSON OBJECTIVE
Identify ways to act ethically and responsibly.

TERMS TO KNOW
ethical: related to behaving in the right way or a good way
integrity: the quality of having good morals; the quality of being honest and trustworthy
morals: strong beliefs or personal rules about how to act in an ethical way
responsible: reliable and trustworthy

GOES WELL WITH LESSONS:
15, 45, 96

21st Century Activities ... Each done in under 21 minutes

PRACTICE
Playing Both Parts
Write on the board: *You lose $20 and someone finds it; OR Your friend wants to come over to hang out while you're babysitting a younger sibling.* Have pairs act out one of these scenes.
- Have students act out their scenes to show both responsible and irresponsible actions.
- After students have played the parts, ask them to describe how they felt about the effects of the irresponsible actions.
- As a class, discuss what values the students showed when they acted responsibly or irresponsibly.

☐ CLASS WORK ☐ HOMEWORK
☐ EXTRA CREDIT ☐ PROJECT

APPLY
Trust Me!
Individuals complete **Activity Sheet 106**.
- Students read, then complete the Mind Map for *Apply*.
- Students respond to the questions for *Write* in their **Journal (p. W3)**.

Possible Answers APPLY: Responsible/ Effect: Tell the teacher the answer key is in full view. / The teacher will hide the key and no one will get the answers. **Irresponsible/ Effect:** Take the answer key. / Ace the test dishonestly, possibly affecting the grading curve. **WRITE:** Answers will vary based on personal experience.

☐ CLASS WORK ☐ HOMEWORK
☐ EXTRA CREDIT ☐ PROJECT

EXTEND
Connect to Environmental Literacy
Many people around the world work hard to help the environment. Information about the environment is spread because many people believe we need to act responsibly and care for the environment.

Identify an environmental problem, such as the hole in the ozone layer or the need for a local paper recycling program. Create text and choose images for a new Web page, giving information about the issue and encouraging people to act responsibly and do the right thing.

☐ CLASS WORK ☐ HOMEWORK
☐ EXTRA CREDIT ☐ PROJECT

Unit 3 People Skills

NAME _____ DATE _____

Trust Me!

106 WHY TRY? Because— My actions affect others!

INVESTIGATE ▶ Find out what it means to act responsibly.

Acting responsibly means that you're not just a good student—you're a good citizen. When you demonstrate good morals, showing that you know the difference between right and wrong, you help make your school and your town a better place. Look at the example below.

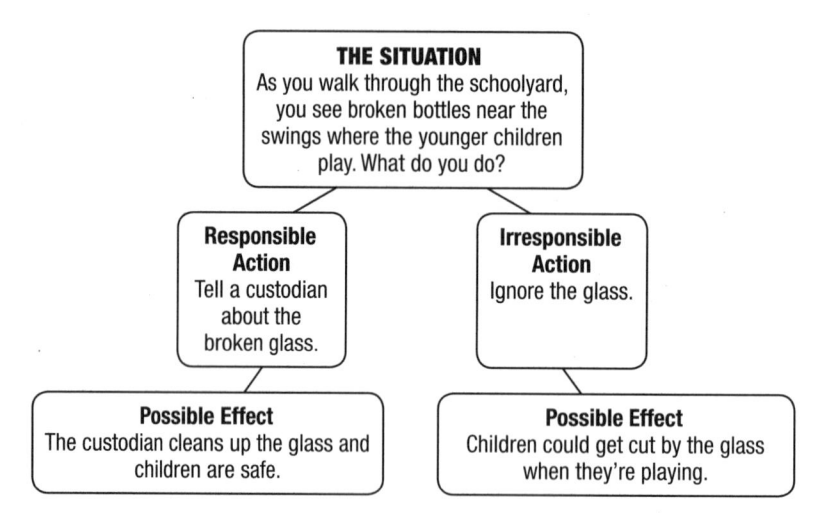

THE SITUATION
As you walk through the schoolyard, you see broken bottles near the swings where the younger children play. What do you do?

Responsible Action
Tell a custodian about the broken glass.

Irresponsible Action
Ignore the glass.

Possible Effect
The custodian cleans up the glass and children are safe.

Possible Effect
Children could get cut by the glass when they're playing.

APPLY ▶ Think carefully about responsible and irresponsible reactions to the situation described below. Fill in the Mind Map.

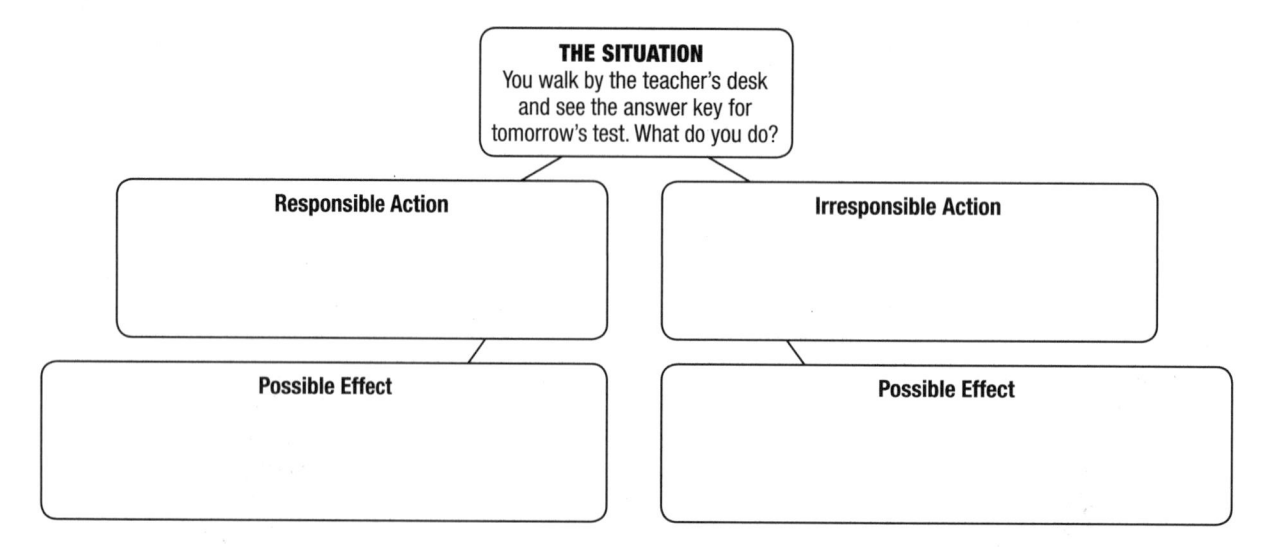

THE SITUATION
You walk by the teacher's desk and see the answer key for tomorrow's test. What do you do?

Responsible Action

Irresponsible Action

Possible Effect

Possible Effect

WRITE ▶ Reply to the questions in your Journal.

Think about a time when you acted responsibly. What happened, and how did your actions affect others? What might have happened in that situation if you had acted irresponsibly?

Lesson 106 Acting Responsibly   © 2011 Saddleback Educational Publishing

Inspiring Others to Do Good Work

107

INTRODUCE THINK ABOUT IT *How can seeing other people do terrific work make us want to do the same?*

TEACH LISTEN UP! People who work hard **inspire** others to do their very best. These are often **selfless** people who share their time, talent, and money with those in need:
- a volunteer who tutors kids after school
- a lawyer who helps poor people free of charge
- a group of kids who turn a weedy lot into a vegetable garden

What do inspiring people have in common? They think of others before they think of themselves. Their selflessness and good examples encourage other people to do the same.

LET'S EXPLORE Name as many people who set good examples as possible.
- As a class, spend 1–3 minutes naming people who set good examples. Encourage students to name both famous people and people from their local community, such as the person who runs a local homeless shelter or a celebrity who fights for a cause.
- Identify which people, places, or groups these individuals choose to help.
- Then ask: *Which of these people or projects is most inspiring to you?* Discuss.

TIME FOR Q & A Discover more about people who do good work: Wendy Kopp/Teach for America; Paul Farmer/Partners In Health; Denis Hayes/Earth Day; John Muir/Sierra Club.

▸ *How did Wendy Kopp want to help students?* She wanted to get good teachers into schools where students needed help.

▸ *Which people does Paul Farmer's organization help?* very poor people in several countries

▸ *Why did Denis Hayes want to start Earth Day?* He wanted to teach people the need to care for the environment.

▸ *How did John Muir protect the environment?* He helped to set up national parks.

REFLECT *How can we inspire other people by our own example?*

INSPIRING OTHERS TO DO GOOD WORK

LESSON OBJECTIVE
Identify and apply ways to set good examples for others.

TERMS TO KNOW
inspire: to influence or encourage by example
selfless: unselfish, giving of oneself

GOES WELL WITH LESSONS:
30, 44, 103

21st Century Activities ... Each done in under 21 minutes

PRACTICE
Problem or Opportunity?
When disasters strike, many people, including children and teens, respond to help those in need. Have students research people who helped disaster victims.
- Assign a disaster to each group, such as Hurricane Katrina or the 2010 Haiti earthquake.
- Groups research information about how people helped the victims.
- Groups share their information with the class, perhaps focusing on one particular group or person they found most inspiring.
- Discuss how the various helpers might have inspired others.

☐ CLASS WORK ☐ HOMEWORK
☐ EXTRA CREDIT ☐ PROJECT

APPLY
Two Inspiring Examples
Groups of 3–4 complete **Activity Sheet 107.**
- Students read and answer items 1 and 2.
- For *Collaborate,* provide Internet resources, if necessary.
- Encourage groups to think creatively about community needs. Groups should present to the class together.

Possible Answers 1. *They wanted to help others.* **2.** *Their work helped soldiers during wars and many other people.*
COLLABORATE: 3. *Presentations will vary.*

☐ CLASS WORK ☐ HOMEWORK
☐ EXTRA CREDIT ☐ PROJECT

EXTEND
Connect to Health Literacy
Many people do not have access to health care when they need it. Often, volunteer organizations offer clinics or other services to help people who cannot afford care.

Locate an example of a local organization that gives health care to people in need. Create an ad for it explaining how their work helps others and should inspire others in the community. Include an image or images in the ad. Make the ad on poster board or on a computer.

☐ CLASS WORK ☐ HOMEWORK
☐ EXTRA CREDIT ☐ PROJECT

Unit 3 People Skills   69

Two Inspiring Examples

INVESTIGATE Read about two famous nurses who made a difference for others.

107 WHY TRY? Because— I can set a good example!

Two of history's most famous nurses are Clara Barton and Florence Nightingale. Both women lived and worked in the 1800s.

Clara Barton was an American. She began nursing during the Civil War. The suffering of wounded soldiers upset her. For that reason, she offered to go to the front lines of battle. People called her the "Angel of the Battlefield" because of the way she helped the injured. After the war ended, she visited Europe. There, she saw how the International Red Cross helped disaster victims. Barton worked to create the American Red Cross. She became its first president.

In Great Britain, another nurse was doing similar work. Florence Nightingale had always wanted to care for those who were sick. She took her nursing skills to a war in Turkey. There, she became "Lady-in-Chief" of nurses. She made nightly hospital rounds, carrying a lantern from bed to bed. Grateful soldiers called her the "Lady with the Lamp." Because of her work, hospital death rates dropped from 40% to 2%. Florence Nightingale became an authority on nursing methods. She advised the United States on its Civil War hospitals.

CLARA BARTON | FLORENCE NIGHTINGALE

RECALL Think about the passage you read, then respond.

1. Why did Barton and Nightingale want to become nurses?

_____

2. Whom did their work help?

_____

COLLABORATE Work with a group.

Think of ways that people in your own city or state might need help. Research current programs available that help them. If no programs help the people, create ideas for ways they could be helped. In an oral report, present the information to the class. Include visual aids. If possible, use software to create a presentaton with notes about the information.

Lesson 107 Inspiring Others to Do Good Work © 2011 Saddleback Educational Publishing

Living by a Code of Ethics

108

INTRODUCE **THINK ABOUT IT** *You make choices every day between good and bad, and right and wrong. How do those choices show your code of ethics?*

TEACH **LISTEN UP!** Ethics are rules you set for yourself. When you see something happen that you think is not right, you're responding to you own set of **values.** For example,

- It's not *honest* to cheat on an exam.
- It's not *fair* to get extra time on a project if other people don't.
- It's not *respectful* to interrupt an older person when she's talking.
- It's not *responsible* to leave a young child alone.

Honesty, fairness, respectfulness, and responsibility are just some of the values that can go into a person's code of ethics. When you're faced with an ethical decision, ask yourself: *What are my values? How does this choice fit into my value system?*

LET'S EXPLORE Brainstorm examples of values.

- As a class, spend 1–5 minutes listing values that could make up a code of ethics, e.g., honesty, friendship, responsibility, trustworthiness, personal safety, respect.
- Write the list of values on the board and ask class members to discuss whether any values on the list are more important to them than others.
- Ask: *What would you do in a situation in which two values were in conflict?*

TIME FOR Q & A Discuss with the class how they live by their important values.

▶ *When might it be hard to be honest?* when being honest would hurt someone's feelings

▶ *Why do I have to be responsible? It's not fun.* Being ethical isn't always fun, but it's right.

REFLECT *Being ethical is always in style, because important values never change.*

LIVING BY A CODE OF ETHICS

LESSON OBJECTIVE
Examine personal values and use them to make ethical choices.

TERMS TO KNOW
ethics: a set of moral principles; rules showing the difference between right and wrong
values: beliefs of a person or group

GOES WELL WITH LESSONS:
23, 45, 96

21st Century Activities ... Each done in under 21 minutes

PRACTICE
Create the Code of Ethics
Small groups create a Code of Ethics for the classroom.

- Students work in small groups to pick five values that matter most to them.
- Groups should explain those values with examples or illustrations from their own experience.
- Groups write down their ideas and present their Code of Ethics to the class. As a class, vote on the top 10 values that should be used for a class Code of Ethics.

☐ CLASS WORK ☐ HOMEWORK
☐ EXTRA CREDIT ☐ PROJECT

APPLY
Tough Decisions
Pairs complete **Activity Sheet 108.**

- Students read the questions for decision-making and the example situation.
- Pairs complete the flow chart for *Evaluate* and then write a script for one of the two situations on the page. If time allows, pairs can act out their scene for the class.

Possible Answers EVALUATE: Box **1.** friendship, integrity, honesty, etc. Box **2.** Toi should talk to Rosa about her feelings, and they can work it out together. **WRITE:** Scripts will vary.

☐ CLASS WORK ☐ HOMEWORK
☐ EXTRA CREDIT ☐ PROJECT

EXTEND
Connect to Civic Literacy
Consider the ethics involved when people run for a public office, such as mayor or President of the United States. These people often have to balance their values against what they know voters want to hear.

Pretend you are running for President of the United States. Make a campaign poster to convince people to vote for you. On the poster, list the values you hold dear. Also include certain actions you might want to take to help Americans—actions that show your values. Include an image on the poster, too.

☐ CLASS WORK ☐ HOMEWORK
☐ EXTRA CREDIT ☐ PROJECT

Unit 3 People Skills

NAME _____ DATE _____

Tough Decisions

108 WHY TRY? Because— I can make good decisions!

INVESTIGATE Think about how you make ethical decisions.

Every day, you use your values to make small choices and big decisions. Some ethical choices are simple. Other choices may require that you ask yourself *What are my values? How does this choice fit into my value system?* Look at this example:

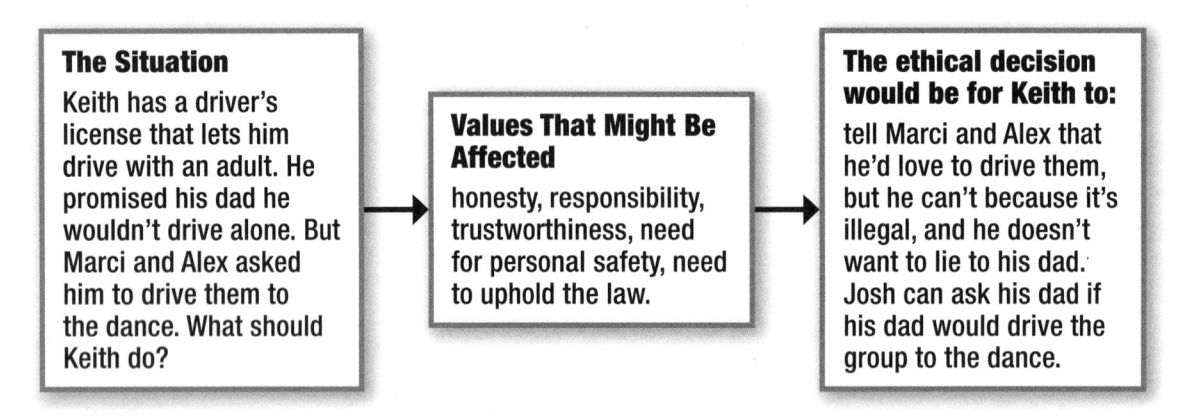

The Situation
Keith has a driver's license that lets him drive with an adult. He promised his dad he wouldn't drive alone. But Marci and Alex asked him to drive them to the dance. What should Keith do?

→

Values That Might Be Affected
honesty, responsibility, trustworthiness, need for personal safety, need to uphold the law.

→

The ethical decision would be for Keith to:
tell Marci and Alex that he'd love to drive them, but he can't because it's illegal, and he doesn't want to lie to his dad. Josh can ask his dad if his dad would drive the group to the dance.

EVALUATE Read the situation below. Then, fill in the rest of the flow chart.

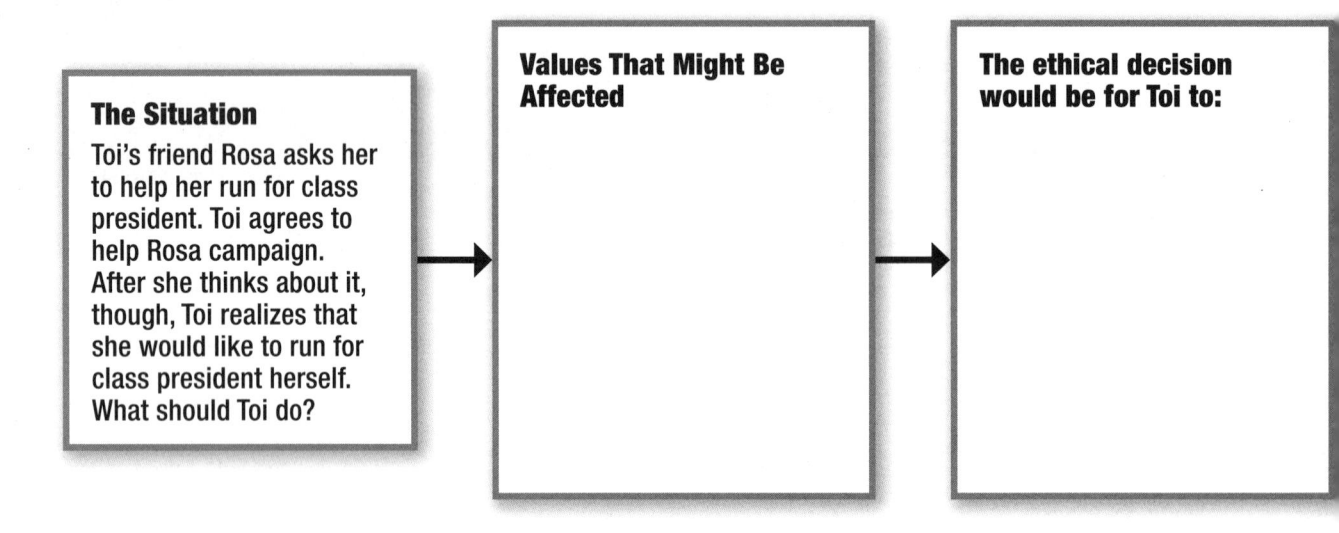

The Situation
Toi's friend Rosa asks her to help her run for class president. Toi agrees to help Rosa campaign. After she thinks about it, though, Toi realizes that she would like to run for class president herself. What should Toi do?

→

Values That Might Be Affected

→

The ethical decision would be for Toi to:

WRITE With a partner, write a script for one of the situations described on this activity sheet. In the script, include the thoughts of Keith or Toi as he or she makes the decision. Also include dialogue between the characters. Be sure that the script shows the ethical decision. If time allows, act out your script in front of the class.

Lesson 108 Living by a Code of Ethics © 2011 Saddleback Educational Publishing

NAME _____ DATE _____

Learning Pathways Survey

Check any boxes that describe you or that you agree are true. Count the number of checks in each box and write the total. Then, add down to get the Grand Total for each column. Circle the Grand Total that is the greatest.

	C	**T**	**W**
1	☐ I like making things. ☐ I have a lot of fun ideas. ☐ I daydream a lot. ☐ I work hard to plan my ideas. ☐ Other people's ideas really interest me. ☐ I think technology is amazing. ☐ Some people think that I'm really ahead of my time. ☐ I like to express myself in creative ways. ☐ Art inspires me. ☐ I can usually tell how others feel. Total checks _____	☐ I like to research things. ☐ Magazines are fun to read. ☐ I can figure out graphs and diagrams. ☐ Concentrating is no problem for me. ☐ Computers will help us even more in the future. ☐ I can work alone or in a team. ☐ I like to find the details that make up the big picture. ☐ Staying current with new technology is important. ☐ I like to take things apart. ☐ I like facts and figures. Total checks _____	☐ I like to be on my own. ☐ I'm good at setting and reaching goals. ☐ I make my own rules. ☐ Doing things myself is faster than explaining it to someone else. ☐ I like discovering new bands. ☐ People are always asking my opinion on the best new movies. ☐ I write in a journal or a blog. ☐ I always plan ahead. ☐ I don't like going with the flow. ☐ Even though I'm independent, I help others when they need it. Total checks _____
2	☐ I like puzzles. ☐ I am good at math. ☐ I use facts to predict what will happen in the future. ☐ Finances are easy to explain. ☐ People trust me with money. ☐ I'd rather read a book than talk. ☐ I always try to turn in my work on time. ☐ Paying attention to the details is key for success. ☐ We shouldn't waste time or money. ☐ I come up with good solutions to problems. Total checks _____	☐ I love computers. ☐ TV commercials are cool to watch. ☐ Watching movies helps me relax. ☐ I like to study the words and designs used in ads. ☐ I watch or read the news daily. ☐ It's important to have the latest technologies and gadgets. ☐ The Internet is a great tool for learning and communicating. ☐ I would be lost without my cell phone and MP3 player. ☐ I like to surf the Web. ☐ Copying music and videos without paying is stealing. Total checks _____	☐ I have a part-time job. ☐ Making money is cool. ☐ I feel comfortable leading others. ☐ I have a lot of good ideas on how to get jobs done. ☐ People come to me to ask how to complete a task in the best way. ☐ I am a good communicator. ☐ I can be patient, but I'm also hardworking. ☐ I am good at resolving conflicts. ☐ I like to save money. ☐ People often ask me for advice. Total checks _____
3	☐ I talk on the phone a lot. ☐ I'm good at explaining things. ☐ My friends listen to me. ☐ Song lyrics are just as, if not more, important than the music. ☐ I like to teach other people how to do things. ☐ Vocabulary words are always easy for me to learn. ☐ I'm a good listener. ☐ I like to speak in front of a group. ☐ I love to debate an issue. ☐ Getting and sharing news is important. Total checks _____	☐ Surfing the Web is fun. ☐ My online friends network has more than 50 people. ☐ Computers are important. ☐ I text a lot. ☐ I like using my computer. ☐ I love to play video games. ☐ My friends and I use social networks. ☐ Essays should be written on a computer not handwritten. ☐ I like using the computer to organize information. ☐ E-mail is better than snail mail. Total checks _____	☐ I like talking to people. ☐ I enjoy playing team sports. ☐ Most people at school consider me to be a friend. ☐ Teamwork is a great way to get things done. ☐ I have my own Web site. ☐ I like to help people reach their goals. ☐ Traveling is a great way to meet people. ☐ Foreign cultures are interesting. ☐ People think I'm outgoing. ☐ I try to stay upbeat. Total checks _____
	Grand Total _____	Grand Total _____	Grand Total _____

© 2011 Saddleback Educational Publishing   Pathway Placement Survey   **W1**

NAME ______________________________ DATE ______________

Graphs

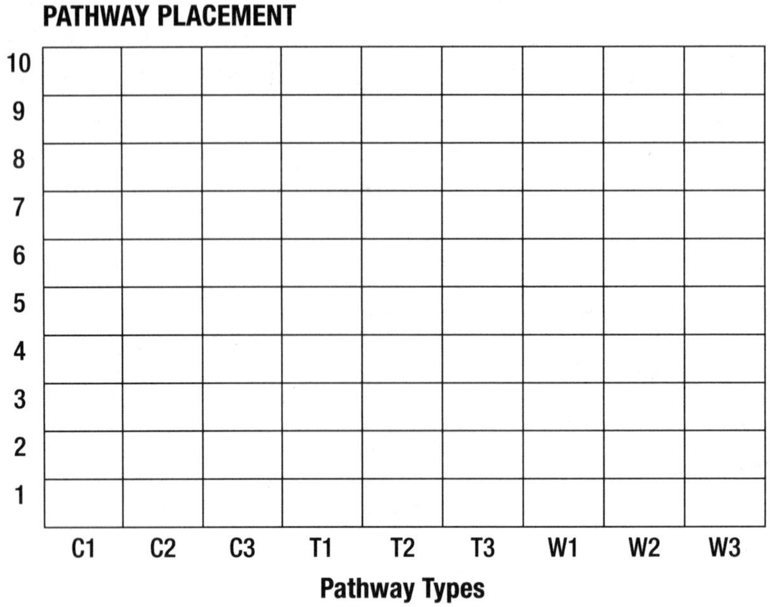

PATHWAY PLACEMENT
10
9
8
7
6
5
4
3
2
1
C1
C2
C3
T1
T2
T3
W1
W2
W3
Pathway Types

Title ______________________________

Y-Axis ______________

X-Axis ______________________

© 2011 Saddleback Educational Publishing

NAME _____ DATE _____

Journal

NAME _____ DATE _____

2-Column Chart

NAME _____ DATE _____

3-Column Chart

NAME _____ **DATE** _____

Checklist

- [ ] _____
- [ ] _____
- [ ] _____
- [ ] _____
- [ ] _____
- [ ] _____
- [ ] _____
- [ ] _____
- [ ] _____
- [ ] _____
- [ ] _____
- [ ] _____
- [ ] _____

NAME _____ DATE _____

Computer Screen

NAME _____ DATE _____

Concept Map

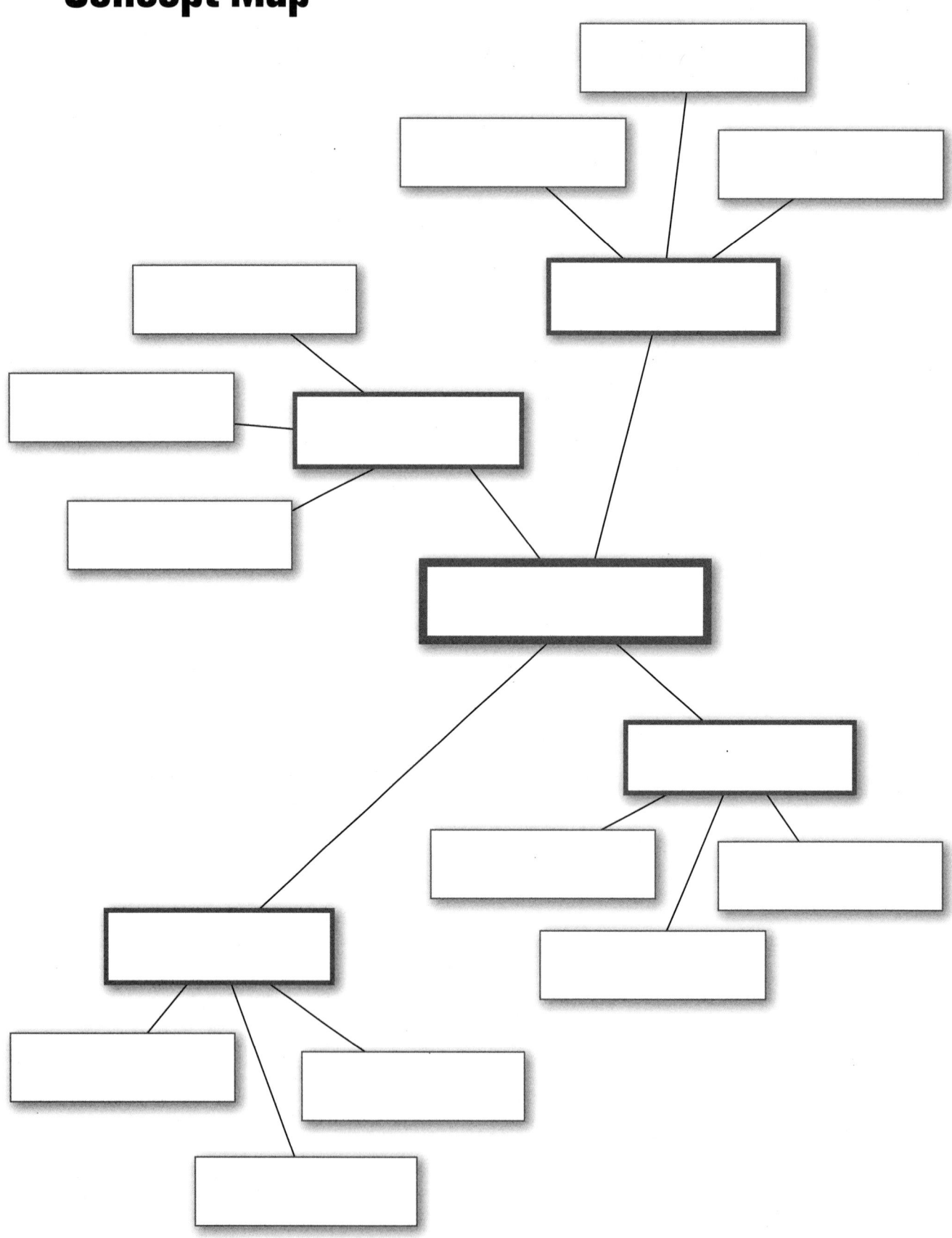

NAME _____ DATE _____

Flow Chart

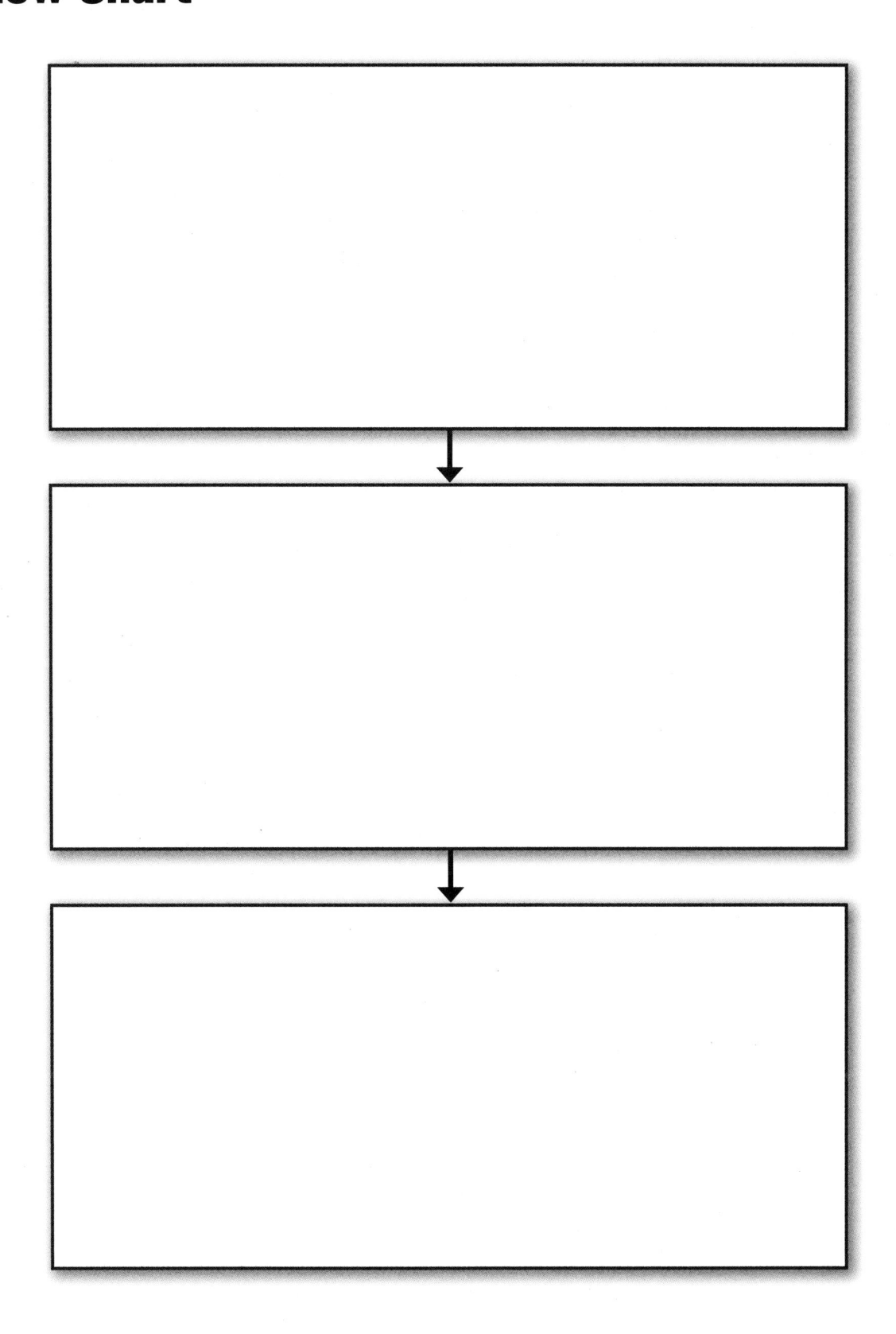

NAME _____ DATE _____

Index/Note Cards

NAME _____ DATE _____

Planner

Title _____

	Sunday, ____	Monday, ____	Tuesday, ____	Wednesday, ____	Thursday, ____	Friday, ____	Saturday, ____
all-day							
9 AM							
10 AM							
11 AM							
NOON							
1 PM							
2 PM							
3 PM							
4 PM							
5 PM							
6 PM							
7 PM							
8 PM							

© 2011 Saddleback Educational Publishing Planner W11

NAME _____ DATE _____

Spreadsheet

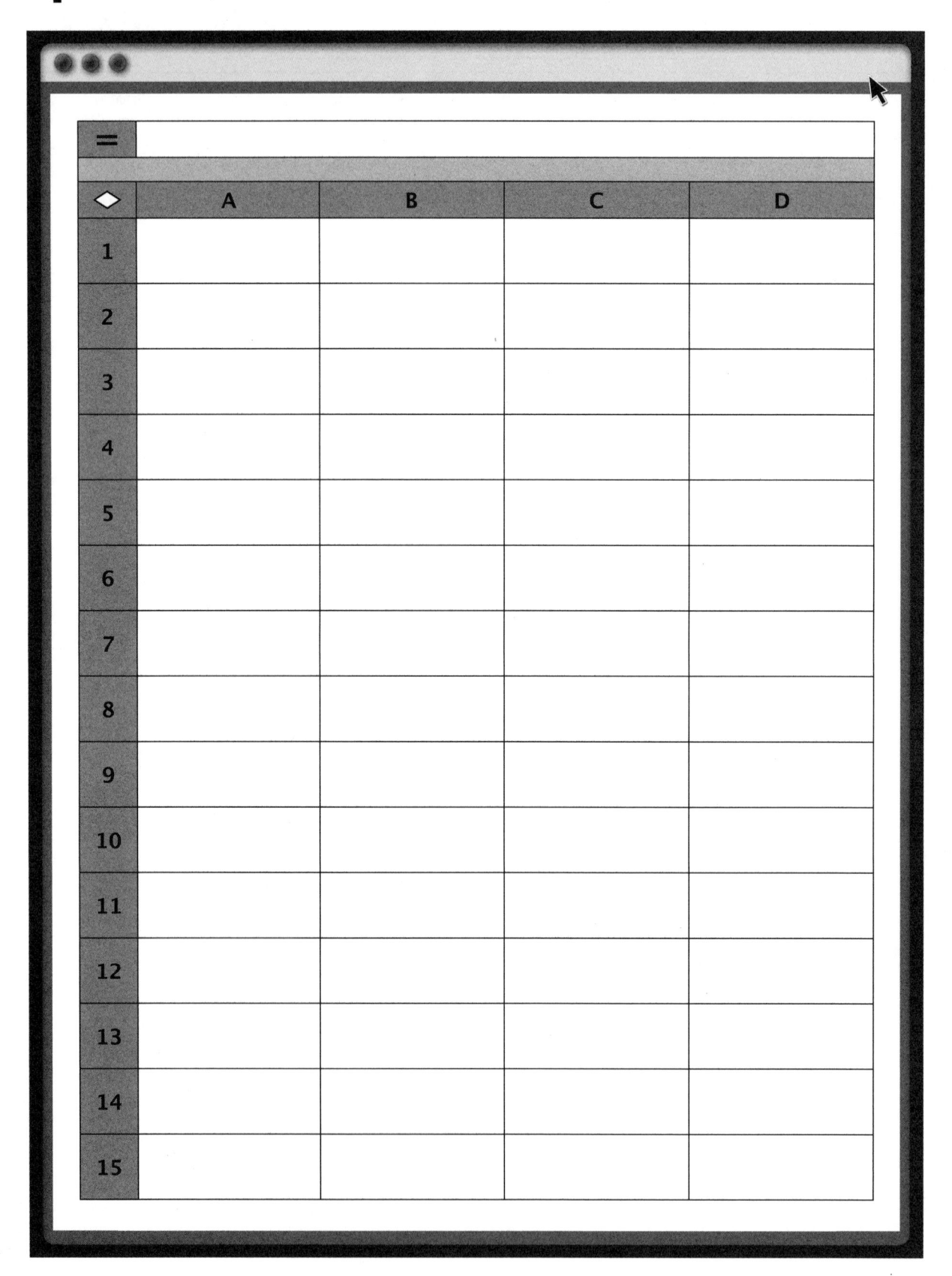

	A	B	C	D
1				
2				
3				
4				
5				
6				
7				
8				
9				
10				
11				
12				
13				
14				
15				

Spreadsheet © 2011 Saddleback Educational Publishing

NAME _____ DATE _____

Storyboard

Storyboard W13

NAME _____ **DATE** _____

Thought Bubble and Speech Balloon

NAME _____ **DATE** _____

Timeline

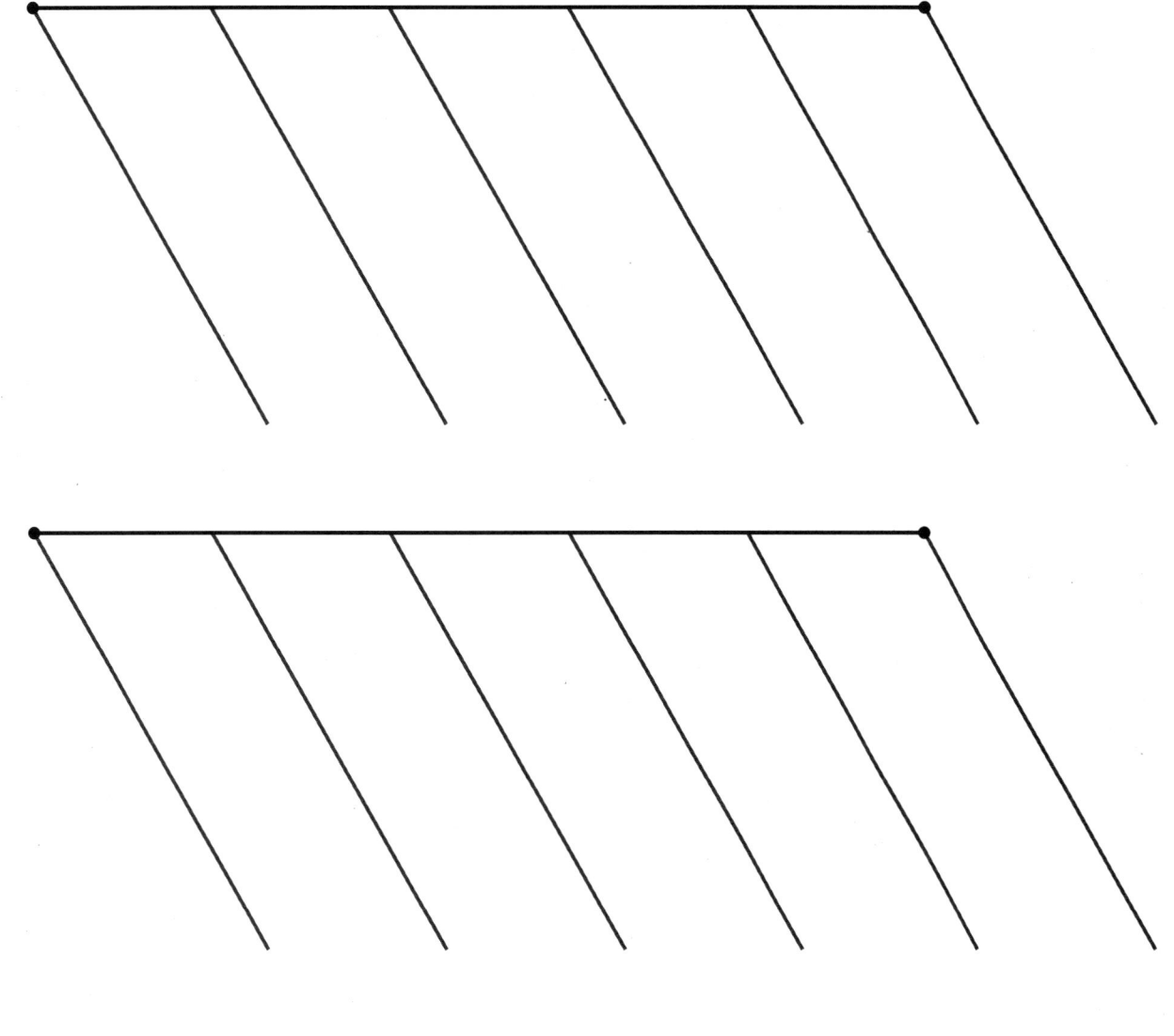

Timeline W15

NAME _____ DATE _____

Venn Diagram

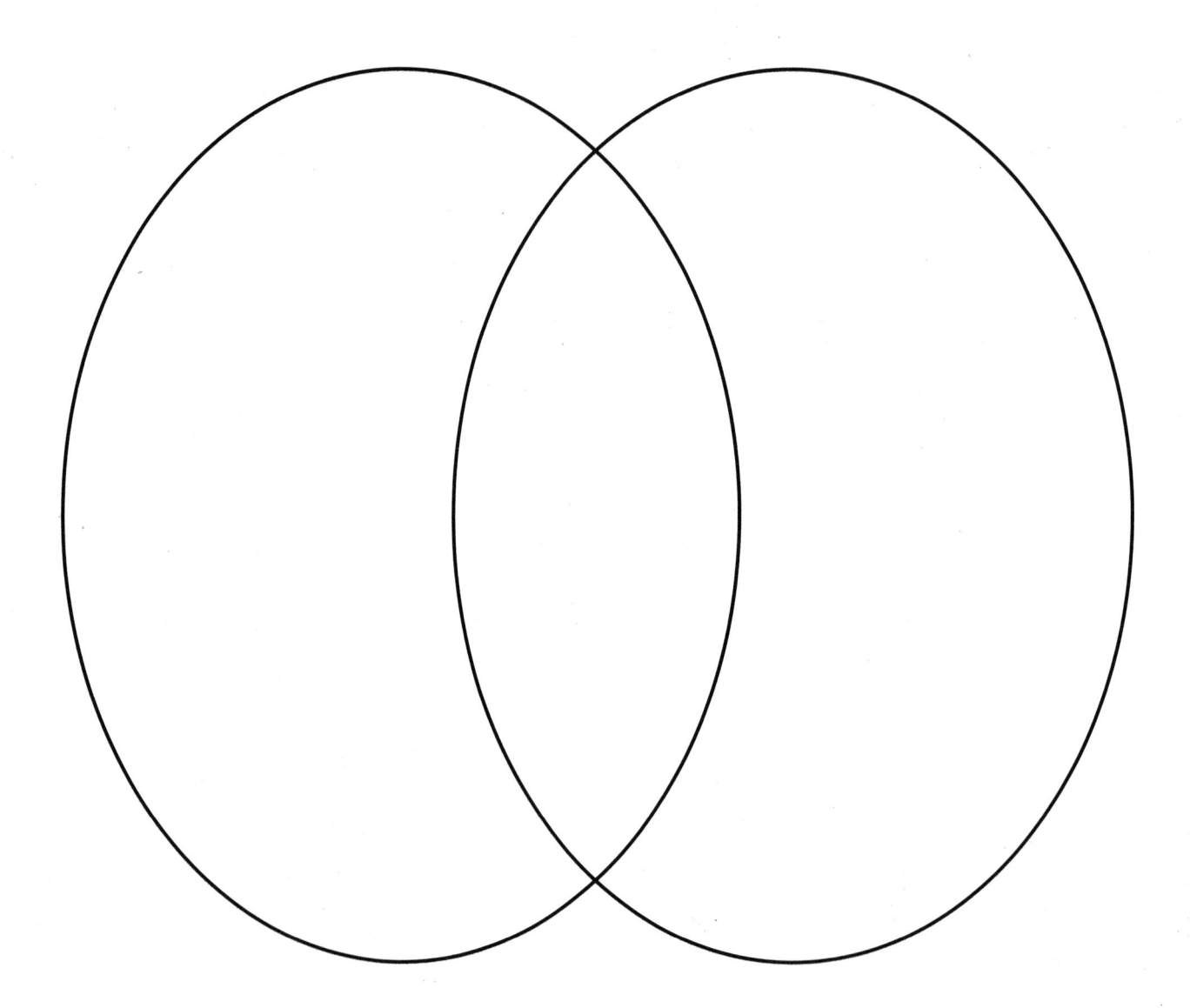

W16 Venn Diagram © 2011 Saddleback Educational Publishing